STEM Labs
for
Middle Grades

Authors: Schyrlet Cameron and Carolyn Craig
Editor: Mary Dieterich
Proofreaders: April Albert and Margaret Brown

COPYRIGHT © 2016 Mark Twain Media, Inc.

ISBN 978-1-62223-595-7

Printing No. CD-404250

Mark Twain Media, Inc., Publishers
Distributed by Carson-Dellosa Publishing LLC

Table of Contents

Table of Contents (cont.)

To the Teacher

STEM is an acronym for Science, Technology, Engineering, and Mathematics. STEM education is an initiative designed to get students interested in these career fields. STEM learning emphasizes students gaining the knowledge and developing the skills needed for a 21st-century workforce.

STEM Labs for Middle Grades provides fun and meaningful integrated activities designed to cultivate an interest in the topics in the STEM fields. Students actively engage in solving real-world problems using scientific inquiry, content knowledge, and technological design. All the activities in this book are lab investigations that support the national standards.

This book contains 52 challenging STEM lab activities. Each activity asks students to solve a problem. Key components of every activity are creativity, teamwork, communication, and critical thinking. Student mastery of each activity is evaluated by both teachers and students using the STEM Task Rubric and the STEM Self-Evaluation. Each activity requires students to:

- **Research:** Students find out what is already known about the topic being investigated.

- **Collaborate:** Students complete activities in collaborative groups. They are encouraged to communicate openly, support each other, and respect contributions of members as they pool perspectives and experiences toward solving a problem.

- **Design:** Students use creativity and imagination to design an object, process, model, or system. Students test the design, record data, and analyze and interpret results.

- **Reflect:** Students think back on the process in a way that further promotes higher-order thinking.

STEM Labs for Middle Grades is written for classroom teachers, parents, and students. This book can be used to supplement existing curriculum or enhance after school or summer school programs.

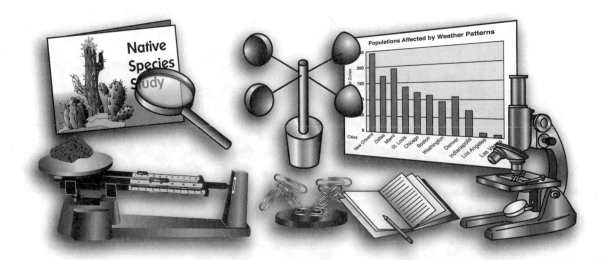

STEM Education

The STEMs of Learning: **Science**, **Technology**, **Engineering**, and **Mathematics** is an initiative designed to get students interested in these career fields. In 2009, the National Academy of Engineering (NAE) and the National Research Council (NRC) reported that there was a lack of focus on the science, technology, engineering, and mathematics (STEM) subjects in K–12 schools. This creates concerns about the competitiveness of the United States in the global market and the development of a workforce with the knowledge and skills needed to address technical and technological issues.

STEM Education	
STEM	**Knowledge and Skills Needed to Address Technical and Technological Issues**
Science	**Basic science process skills** include the basic skills of classifying, observing, measuring, inferring, communicating, predicting, manipulating materials, replicating, using numbers, developing vocabulary, questioning, and using cues. **Integrated science skills** (more complex skills) include creating models, formulating a hypothesis, generalizing, identifying and controlling variables, defining operationally, recording and interpreting data, making decisions, and experimenting.
Technology	**Design process** includes identifying and collecting information about everyday problems that can be solved by technology. It also includes generating ideas and requirements for solving the problems.
Engineering	**Design process** includes identifying a problem or design opportunity; proposing designs and possible solutions; implementing the solution; evaluating the solution and its consequences; and communicating the problem, processes, and solution.
Mathematics	**Mathematical skills** include the ability to use problem-solving skills, formulate problems, develop and apply a variety of strategies to solve problems, verify and interpret results, and generalize solutions and strategies to new problems. Students also need to be able to communicate with models, orally, in writing, and with pictures and graphs; reflect and clarify their own thinking; use the skills of reading, listening, and observing to interpret and evaluate ideas; and be able to make conjectures and convincing arguments.

1

Characteristics of a STEM Lesson

STEM education emphasizes a new way of teaching and learning that focuses on hands-on inquiry and open-ended exploration. It allows students with diverse interests, abilities, and experiences to develop skills they will need in the 21st-century workforce. It is a shift away from the teacher presenting information and covering science topics to the teacher guiding and assisting students in problem-solving while encouraging them to take the lead in their own learning.

A STEM Lesson

A good STEM lesson has several characteristics. It starts with a problem that stimulates the curiosity and interest of both girls and boys. A STEM lesson:

- emphasizes hands-on, inquiry-based learning.
- addresses both math and science standards.
- encourages the use of or creation of technology.
- involves the engineering design process.
- stresses collaborative teamwork.

10 Steps in a STEM Lesson

Students are presented with a challenge to design a model, process, or system to solve a problem. They work on the challenge in collaborative teams of three or four students. Each team follows a set of problem-solving steps in order to find a solution.

Step #1:   Research the problem and solutions.

Step #2:   Brainstorm ideas about how to design a model, process, or system to solve the problem.

Step #3:   Draw a diagram of the model, process, or system.

Step #4:   Construct a prototype.

Step #5:   Test the prototype.

Step #6:   Evaluate the performance of the prototype.

Step #7:   Identify how to improve the design of the prototype.

Step #8:   Make the needed changes to the prototype.

Step #9:   Retest and re-evaluate the prototype.

Step #10: Share the results.

Collaborative Learning Teams

Collaborative learning is a successful teaching strategy in which small groups of students, each with different levels of ability and diverse interests and experiences, work together to solve a problem, complete a task, or create a product. Each student is individually accountable for their own work, and the work of the group as a whole is also evaluated.

Benefits of Collaborative Learning

The responsibility for learning is placed squarely on the shoulders of the students. The role of the teacher is to guide and assist the students in the problem-solving process. A collaborative learning environment in the science classroom has many benefits, including:

- engaging students in active learning,
- encouraging students to communication openly,
- motivating students to cooperate and support each other,
- teaching respect for contributions of all members, and
- preparing students for the real world.

Team Dynamics

It is important that the teacher organizes the classroom into teams. Teams should consist of no more than three or four students. Fewer members may limit the diversity of ideas, skills, and approaches to problem-solving.

Assigning Roles

A successful collaborative learning experience requires a division of the workload among the members of a team. The teacher may wish to assign the role of each member of the team as follows:

- **Team Captain** is responsible for keeping the group on-task.

- **Recorder** is responsible for organizing the paperwork and creating drawings, diagrams, or illustrations as needed.

- **Materials Manager** is responsible for gathering the needed materials and supplies for the project.

- **Monitor** is responsible for keeping the work area tidy and for properly storing the project at the end of the class.

STEM

Science: The study of the natural world.

Technology: A product created to solve a problem.

Engineering: The design process used to solve a problem.

Math: The numbers, shapes, and quantities used to solve a problem.

10 Tips for Student Collaboration

1. Respect Each Other and All Ideas

2. No "Put Downs"

3. Be a Good, Active Listener

4. Come Well Prepared for Task Assignment

5. Participate and Contribute During Discussions

6. Support Your Opinions

7. Promote Positive Team-Member Relations

8. Disagree in an Agreeable Manner

9. Encourage Team Members

10. Complete Tasks on Time and With Quality Work

STEM Task Rubric

Task	1	2	3	4	
Research	Demonstrates no research/inquiry; No information cited	Demonstrates some research/inquiry; Some information cited	Demonstrates research/inquiry; Most information cited	Demonstrates planned research/inquiry that lead to informed decisions; All information cited following copyright guidelines	
Model	Drawing has no labels or explanation of strategy	Drawing has some labels and partial explanation of strategy	Drawing has labels and explanation of strategy	Drawing has labels and advanced explanation of strategy	
Results	No records, analysis, or interpretation of test results	Records, analysis, and/ or interpretation of test results incomplete	Records, analysis, and interpretation of test results completed	All records, analysis, and interpretation of test results in organized, accurate manner	
Conclusion	No purpose, brief description of test procedure, or explanation of test results	Purpose, brief description of test procedure, and explanation of test results incomplete	Purpose, brief description of test procedure, and explanation of test results completed	Purpose, brief description of test procedure, and explanation of test results, which demonstrates high-level thinking	
Reflection	Reflection not completed	Reflection partially completed	Reflection completed	Reflection completed with thoughtful insight into team's choices	
Evaluation	Self-evaluation not completed	Self-evaluation partially completed	Self-evaluation completed	Self-evaluation completed with thoughtful insights about behavior and performance as a team member	

Teacher Comments:

STEM Self-Evaluation Rubric

Directions: Circle the description in each category that you believe best describes your behavior and performance during the assigned task.

Category	1	2	3	4
Attitude	Often critical of the project or the work of other members in the group. Negative attitude about the task.	Sometimes critical of the project or the work of other members in the group. Usually positive attitude about the task.	Rarely critical of the project or the work of other members in the group. Mostly positive attitude about the task.	Never critical of the project or the work of other members in the group. Always positive attitude about the task.
Work Quality	Presents work that needs to be redone by others to ensure quality.	Presents work that occasionally needs to be redone by others to ensure quality.	Presents work of high quality.	Presents work of the highest quality.
Problem-solving	Lets others do the work. Does not try to help solve problems.	Does not suggest solutions, but tries solutions suggested by team members.	Improves solutions suggested by team members.	Actively looks for and suggests solutions to problems.
Contributions	Seldom provides helpful ideas when participating in group and class discussion. Refuses to participate.	Sometimes provides helpful ideas when participating in group and class discussion. An agreeable member who does what is required.	Frequently provides helpful ideas when participating in group and class discussion. Strong member who tries hard.	Regularly provides helpful ideas when participating in group and class discussion. Leader who contributes a lot of effort.
Task Focus	Seldom focuses on task and what needs to be done. Lets others do the work.	Sometimes focuses on task and what needs to be done. Other team members must prod and remind this person to stay on task.	Focuses on task and what needs to be done. Reliable team member.	Constantly focuses on task and what needs to be done. Very self-directed.

Student Comments:

Reflection: Team's Choice and Design

Name: _____ Date: _____

Title of Lab Task: _____

One thing I didn't expect from this investigation was _____

_____

_____

_____

If I want to get better at scientific investigation, I need to _____

_____

_____

_____

The one thing I would improve on if I was doing this investigation again would be _____

_____

_____

_____

The one thing I would like to learn more about after doing this investigation is _____

_____

_____

_____

Having carried out this investigation, I realize that _____

_____

_____

_____

The easiest part of this investigation was _____

_____

_____

_____

The hardest part of this investigation was _____

_____

_____

_____

From completing this investigation, I now understand _____

_____

_____

_____

Lighthouse

Task: Design a lighthouse that will light when you switch on electricity.

What You Should Know

A **lighthouse** is a type of structure designed to emit light. The light is used to warn boats and ships of marine hazards and to allow navigators to determine their position at night.

Steps to Follow

Work with a team to complete the steps listed below. A team will have 3 or 4 members.

Step 1:   Research energy, electricity, electrical circuits, and lighthouse designs.
Step 2:   Brainstorm ideas about how you might design a lighthouse.
Step 3:   Draw a diagram of your lighthouse.
Step 4:   Construct your lighthouse.
Step 5:   Test your lighthouse.
Step 6:   Evaluate the performance of your lighthouse.
Step 7:   Identify how to improve the design of your lighthouse.
Step 8:   Make the needed changes.
Step 9:   Retest and re-evaluate your lighthouse.
Step 10: Share your results.

Terminology You Should Know

battery: an energy source

conductor: a material capable of transmitting electric current

current electricity: the movement of electrons, which creates a flow of electricity

electrical circuit: a complete path through which electrons flow from an energy source, through a conducting wire and appliance, and back to the energy source

insulator: a material capable of preventing the transfer of electricity

potential energy: the stored energy an object has because of its position, rather than its motion

series circuit: a circuit that has a single path for electric current to flow

switch: a device used to open and close circuits

Materials You May Need

- two-liter bottle   • tape   • cardboard
- scissors   • wire   • paper clips
- battery   • bulb   • shoe box
- bulb holder   • glue
- clear plastic or glass container

Task Requirements

1. <u>Research</u>: A one- to two-page paper summarizing your research on energy, electricity, electrical circuits, and lighthouses. Cite your sources. Your paper may include two pictures.
2. <u>Model</u>: A labeled drawing of your lighthouse design and explanation of your strategy.
3. <u>Results</u>: A record, analysis, and interpretation of test results.
4. <u>Conclusion</u>: A summary of the task and what actually happened. It should include the purpose, a brief description of the test procedure, and explanation of results.
5. <u>Reflection</u>: Think about your team's choices and your lighthouse design. Then complete the "Reflection" handout.
6. <u>Evaluation</u>: Think about your behavior and performance as a team member. Then complete the "Self-Evaluation Rubric."

Flashlight

Task: Design a flashlight that will light when you switch on electricity.

What You Should Know

Flashlights have been around since the late 1800s. Miniature incandescent electric light bulb and dry cell invention made the first battery-powered flashlights possible. Most flashlights today use incandescent lamps or light-emitting diodes and use disposable or rechargeable batteries.

Steps to Follow

Work with a team to complete the steps listed below. A team will have 3 or 4 members.

Step 1:   Research electricity, electrical circuits, and flashlights.
Step 2:   Brainstorm ideas about how you might design your flashlight.
Step 3:   Draw a diagram of your flashlight.
Step 4:   Construct your flashlight.
Step 5:   Test your flashlight.
Step 6:   Evaluate the performance of your flashlight.
Step 7:   Identify how to improve the design of your flashlight.
Step 8:   Make the needed changes.
Step 9:   Retest and re-evaluate your flashlight design.
Step 10: Share your results.

Terminology You Should Know

battery: an energy source

conductor: a material capable of transmitting electricity

current electricity: the movement of electrons, which creates a flow of electricity

electrical circuit: a complete path through which electrons flow from an energy source, through a conducting wire and appliance, and back to the energy source

insulator: a material capable of preventing the transfer of electricity

potential energy: the stored energy an object has because of its position, rather than its motion

series circuit: a circuit that has a single path for electric current to flow

switch: a device used to open and close circuits

Materials You May Need

- one-liter plastic bottle
- two batteries
- bulb with holder
- scissors
- paper clip
- glue
- two brass paper brads
- foil
- tape
- wire

Task Requirements

1. Research: A one- to two-page paper summarizing your research on electricity, electrical circuits, and flashlights. Cite your sources. Your paper may include two pictures.
2. Model: A labeled drawing of your flashlight design and explanation of your strategy.
3. Results: A record, analysis, and interpretation of test results.
4. Conclusion: A summary of the task and what actually happened. It should include the purpose, a brief description of the test procedure, and explanation of results.
5. Reflection: Think about your team's choices and your flashlight design. Then complete the "Reflection" handout.
6. Evaluation: Think about your behavior and performance as a team member. Then complete the "Self-Evaluation Rubric."

Security Alarm

Task: Design a simple security alarm that will ring a buzzer when stepped on by someone entering through a door.

What You Should Know

Security alarms are used for protection against theft as well as personal protection against intruders.

Facts
- Electricity will flow from a battery, if it has a path, such as a wire, to move along.
- Electricity can only move in one direction.

Steps to Follow

Work with a team to complete the steps listed below. A team will have 3 or 4 members.

Step 1:   Research electricity and electrical circuits.
Step 2:   Brainstorm ideas about how you might design a security alarm.
Step 3:   Draw a diagram of your security alarm.
Step 4:   Construct your security alarm.
Step 5:   Test and evaluate your alarm.
Step 6:   Identify how to improve your alarm design.
Step 7:   Make the needed changes.
Step 8:   Retest and re-evaluate your security alarm.
Step 9:   Share your results.

Terminology You Should Know

battery: an energy source

conductor: a material that allows an electric current to pass through it

current electricity: the movement of electrons, which creates a flow of electricity

electrical circuit: a complete path through which electrons flow from an energy source, through a conducting wire and appliance, and back to the energy source

insulator: a material capable of preventing the transfer of electricity

potential energy: the stored energy an object has because of its position, rather than its motion

series circuit: a circuit that has a single path for electric current to flow

switch: a device used to open and close circuits

Materials You May Need

- battery
- wire
- thin cardboard
- aluminum foil
- tape
- buzzer

Task Requirements

1. <u>Research</u>: A one- to two-page paper summarizing your research on electricity and electrical circuits. Cite your sources. Your paper may include two pictures.
2. <u>Model</u>: A labeled drawing of your security alarm and explanation of your strategy.
3. <u>Results</u>: A record, analysis, and interpretation of test results.
4. <u>Conclusion</u>: A summary of the task and what actually happened. It should include the purpose, a brief description of the test procedure, and explanation of results.
5. <u>Reflection</u>: Think about your team's choices and your alarm design. Then complete the "Reflection" handout.
6. <u>Evaluation</u>: Think about your behavior and performance as a team member. Then complete the "Self-Evaluation Rubric."

Electronic Quiz Game

Task: Use your knowledge of electricity to design a five-question-and-answer electronic quiz game that will light a bulb when a player chooses the correct answer.

What You Should Know

Turning on the lights in a room requires the use of a circuit. Radios, computers, and nearly all electrical devices use circuits.

Steps to Follow

Work with a team to complete the steps listed below. A team will have 3 or 4 members.

Step 1: Research energy, electricity, and electrical circuits.
Step 2: Brainstorm ideas about how to design a game board that will light a bulb when a player chooses the correct answer.
Step 3: Draw a diagram of your game board.
Step 4: Construct your game board.
Step 5: Test and evaluate your game.
Step 6: Identify how to improve your game design.
Step 7: Make the needed changes.
Step 8: Retest and re-evaluate your game.
Step 9: Share your results.

Terminology You Should Know

battery: an energy source

current electricity: the movement of electrons, which creates a flow of electricity

electrical circuit: a complete path through which electrons flow from an energy source, through a conducting wire and appliance, and back to the energy source

conductor: a material capable of transmitting electricity

insulator: a material capable of preventing the transfer of electricity

potential energy: the stored energy an object has because of its position, rather than its motion

series circuit: a circuit that has a single path for electric current to flow

switch: a device used to open and close circuits

Materials You May Need

- manila file folder
- scissors
- bulb holder
- brass paper fasteners
- wire
- glue
- paper
- bulb
- pen
- battery

Task Requirements

1. <u>Research</u>: A one- to two-page paper summarizing your research on energy, electricity, and electrical currents. Cite your sources. Your paper may include two pictures.
2. <u>Model</u>: A labeled drawing of your game board and explanation of your strategy.
3. <u>Results</u>: A record, analysis, and interpretation of test results.
4. <u>Conclusion</u>: A summary of the task and what actually happened. It should include the purpose, a brief description of the test procedure, and explanation of results.
5. <u>Reflection</u>: Think about your team's choices and your game board design. Then complete the "Reflection" handout.
6. <u>Evaluation</u>: Think about your behavior and performance as a team member. Then complete the "Self-Evaluation Rubric."

Electric Motor

Task: Design an electric motor that will make a compass needle spin.

What You Should Know

Electric motors turn electricity into motion. In this process, electrical energy is converted into mechanical energy. Many items found in your home, like washing machines, dryers, and refrigerators, have a motor. They use electricity and magnetism to produce motion.

Steps to Follow

Work with a team to complete the steps listed below. A team will have 3 or 4 members.

Step 1: Research electrical motors, electricity, and magnetism.
Step 2: Brainstorm ideas about how you might design an electric motor that will make a compass needle spin.
Step 3: Draw a diagram of your motor.
Step 4: Construct your motor.
Step 5: Test and evaluate the performance of your motor.
Step 6: Identify how to improve the design of your motor.
Step 7: Make the needed changes.
Step 8: Retest and re-evaluate your motor.
Step 9: Share your results.

Terminology You Should Know

battery: an energy source

electrical current: the amount of electric charge that moves past a certain point each second

electromagnet: a magnet made by wrapping a current-carrying wire around an iron core

magnetic field: an area that surrounds a magnet where a magnetic force can be detected

magnetism: the property of attracting metals, producing a magnetic field by a magnet or a conductor carrying an electric current

mechanical energy: the energy an object has because of its motion or position

Materials You May Need

- Materials to be determined by students through their research

Task Requirements

1. <u>Research</u>: A one- to two-page paper summarizing your research on electrical motors, electricity, and magnetism. Cite your sources. Your paper may include two pictures.
2. <u>Model</u>: A labeled drawing of your motor design and explanation of your strategy.
3. <u>Results</u>: A record, analysis, and interpretation of test results.
4. <u>Conclusion</u>: A summary of the task and what actually happened. It should include the purpose, a brief description of the test procedure, and explanation of results.
5. <u>Reflection</u>: Think about your team's choices and the design of your motor. Then complete the "Reflection" handout.
6. <u>Evaluation</u>: Think about your behavior and performance as a team member. Then complete the "Self-Evaluation Rubric."

Coin Tester

Task: Design a coin tester that will separate coins from steel washers.

What You Should Know

Vending machines have been around for a long time and dispense a variety of products for the consumer. Manual coin-operated vending machines are designed to detect real and fake coins.

Steps to Follow

Work with a team to complete the steps listed below. A team will have 3 or 4 members.

Step 1: Research coin-operated vending machines and magnetism.
Step 2: Brainstorm ideas about how you might design a coin tester.
Step 3: Draw a diagram of your coin tester.
Step 4: Construct your coin tester.
Step 5: Test your coin tester.
Step 6: Evaluate the performance of your coin tester.
Step 7: Identify how to improve the design of your coin tester.
Step 8: Make the needed changes.
Step 9: Retest and re-evaluate your coin tester.
Step 10: Share your results.

Terminology You Should Know

magnet: an object that attracts iron or steel

magnetic metal: a solid such as a rock or piece of metal that has the property of attracting iron or steel

non-magnetic metal: a metal that is not ferrous, including alloys that do not contain significant amounts of iron

Materials You May Need

- shoe box
- various coins
- steel washers
- cardboard strips
- bar magnet (2 cm wide)
- tape
- scissors
- pencil
- box knife

Task Requirements

1. Research: A one- to two-page paper summarizing your research on coin-operated machines and magnetism. Cite your sources. Your paper may include two pictures.
2. Model: A labeled drawing of your coin tester design and explanation of your strategy.
3. Results: A record, analysis, and interpretation of test results.
4. Conclusion: A summary of the task and what actually happened. It should include the purpose, a brief description of the test procedure, and explanation of results.
5. Reflection: Think about your team's choices and the design of your coin tester. Then complete the "Reflection" handout.
6. Evaluation: Think about your behavior and performance as a team member. Then complete the "Self-Evaluation Rubric."

Electromagnetic Crane

Task: Design an electromagnetic crane that will lift a small steel object when you switch on the electricity.

What You Should Know

Electromagnetic cranes are used to lift and move metal objects. They are regularly used in recycling plants and scrap yards due to the high quantity of metal that needs to be moved.

Steps to Follow

Work with a team to complete the steps listed below. A team will have 3 or 4 members.

Step 1: Research electromagnetism and cranes.
Step 2: Brainstorm ideas about how you might design an electromagnetic crane.
Step 3: Draw a diagram of your model.
Step 4: Construct your crane.
Step 5: Test your crane.
Step 6: Evaluate the performance of your electromagnetic crane.
Step 7: Identify how to improve the design of your crane.
Step 8: Make the needed changes.
Step 9: Retest and re-evaluate your crane.
Step 10: Share your results.

Terminology You Should Know

block and tackle: a system of pulleys using more than one movable pulley to reduce the amount of force needed to lift the load

electromagnet: a magnet made by wrapping a current-carrying wire around an iron core

pulley: a simple machine that has one or more wheels with a cable wrapped around them

Materials You May Need

- electromagnet
- iron nail
- cardboard tube
- wire (insulated and non-insulated)
- small cardboard boxes (two square and one long rectangular)
- two thread spools
- strong thread
- tape
- glue
- two pencils
- scissors
- paper clips
- battery

Task Requirements

1. <u>Research</u>: A one- to two-page paper summarizing your research on electromagnetism and cranes. Cite your sources. Your paper may include two pictures.
2. <u>Model</u>: A labeled drawing of your crane design and explanation of your strategy.
3. <u>Results</u>: A record, analysis, and interpretation of test results.
4. <u>Conclusion</u>: A summary of the task and what actually happened. It should include the purpose, a brief description of the test procedure, and explanation of results.
5. <u>Reflection</u>: Think about your team's choices and the design of your electromagnetic crane. Then complete the "Reflection" handout.
6. <u>Evaluation</u>: Think about your behavior and performance as a team member. Then complete the "Self-Evaluation Rubric."

A Rube Goldberg Machine

Task: Apply your knowledge of complex and simple machines to design a Rube Goldberg machine to make an easy task look difficult.

What You Should Know

A Rube Goldberg machine is a device that is designed to perform a simple task in a very complicated way. The machine usually includes a chain reaction.

Steps to Follow

Work with a team to complete the steps listed below. A team will have 3 or 4 members.

Step 1: Research simple machines, Rube Goldberg machines, and Newton's First Law of Motion.

Step 2: Brainstorm to identify the job your machine will perform. Break down the task into at least 20 steps. Use 5 simple machines in your design.

Step 3: Draw a diagram of your Rube Goldberg machine. Number and describe the steps in the machine. Identify the simple machines.

Step 4: Construct your Rube Goldberg machine.

Step 5: Test and evaluate your machine.

Step 6: Identify how to improve your machine and make the needed changes.

Step 7: Retest and re-evaluate your machine.

Step 8: Share your results.

Terminology You Should Know

complex machine: a machine that has two or more simple machines working together to make work easier

force: a push or pull

inertia: the tendency of objects to resist a change in motion

Newton's First Law of Motion: the law states that an object in motion stays in motion while an object at rest stays at rest unless being acted on by an outside force

simple machine: a basic tool that helps people do work easier and faster

Materials You May Need

marbles, dominoes, toy cars, cardboard tubes, scrap lumber, ruler, wheels, gears from toy clock, clothesline, pulley, rope, rubber bands, catapult, magnets, scissors, hand eggbeater, screws, clamps, balloons, tape, PVC pipe, mousetrap, craft sticks, springs, plastic bottles, model airplane propeller, cardboard, plastic tubing, and other materials of your choice

Task Requirements

1. Research: A one- to two-page paper summarizing your research on simple machines, Rube Goldberg machines, and Newton's First Law of Motion and citing your sources. Your paper may include two pictures.

2. Model: A labeled drawing of your Rube Goldberg machine and explanation of steps.

3. Results: A record, analysis, and interpretation of test results.

4. Conclusion: A summary of the task and what actually happened. It should include the purpose, a brief description of the test procedure, and explanation of results.

5. Reflection: Think about your team's choice of task, simple machines, and the order of the steps in the design. Then complete the "Reflection" handout.

6. Evaluation: Think about your behavior and performance as a team member. Then complete the "Self-Evaluation Rubric."

Mousetrap-Powered Vehicle

Task: Design a small vehicle powered by the snapping action of a mousetrap. The vehicle must cover a flat distance of five meters.

What You Should Know

Automotive engineers design new vehicles or look for ways to improve existing automotive engineering technology.

Steps to Follow

Work with a team to complete the steps listed below. A team will have 3 or 4 members.

Step 1: Research automotive engineering and mousetrap racers.

Step 2: Brainstorm ideas for the design of your vehicle. Consider body length and the placement, size, and number of wheels.

Step 3: Draw a diagram of your vehicle.

Step 4: Construct your vehicle.

Step 5: Test your vehicle.

Step 6: Evaluate the performance of your vehicle.

Step 7: Identify how to improve your vehicle.

Step 8: Make the needed changes.

Step 9: Retest and re-evaluate your vehicle.

Step 10: Share your results.

Terminology You Should Know

friction: a force that resists motion

inertia: the tendency of objects to resist change in motion

lever: a rigid bar that is free to rotate about a point called a fulcrum

mechanical energy: the energy an object has because of its motion or position; two kinds: kinetic and potential

Newton's First Law of Motion: the law states that an object in motion stays in motion while an object at rest stays at rest unless being acted on by an outside force

wheel-and-axle: a wheel attached to an axle so that these two parts rotate

Materials You May Need

- wooden snap-back mousetrap
- foam board (usually found at a craft store)
- utility knife (use with adult supervision)
- blank or old CDs and DVDs
- dowel rods with diameter smaller than a straw
- large and small rubber bands
- ruler • string • tape • straws

Task Requirements

1. Research: A one- to two-page paper summarizing your research on automotive engineering and mousetrap racers. Cite your sources. Your paper may include two pictures.
2. Model: A labeled drawing of your vehicle design and explanation of your strategy.
3. Results: A record, analysis, and interpretation of test results.
4. Conclusions: A summary of the task and what actually happened. It should include the purpose, a brief description of the test procedure, and explanation of results.
5. Reflection: Think about the design of your vehicle. Then complete the "Reflection" handout.
6. Evaluation: Think about your behavior and performance as a team member. Then complete the "Self-Evaluation Rubric."

Balloon-Powered Racer

Task: Design a balloon-powered racer that will travel five meters. The racer must have four wheels and be powered with only one balloon.

What You Should Know

A balloon-powered racer works on the same principle that makes real rocket engines work in space. The engine pushes out hot gases from the combustion inside, and that pushes the rocket forward into space.

Steps to Follow

Work with a team to complete the steps listed below. A team will have 3 or 4 members.

Step 1: Research Newton's Third Law of Motion and balloon-powered racers.

Step 2: Brainstorm ideas about how you might design a balloon-powered racer that would travel five meters.

Step 3: Draw a diagram of your racer.

Step 4: Construct your racer.

Step 5: Test your racer.

Step 6: Evaluate performance of your balloon-powered racer.

Step 7: Identify how to improve the design of your racer.

Step 8: Make the needed changes.

Step 9: Retest and revaluate your racer.

Step 10: Share your results.

Terminology You Should Know

action: a force (push or pull) that causes an equal but opposite force

friction: a force that resists motion

motion: the act of moving from one place to another

Newton's Third Law of Motion: the law states that for every action there is an equal and opposite reaction

reaction: a force (push or pull) in the opposite direction caused by an action force

Materials You May Need

- styrofoam meat tray
- small plastic stirrer straws (round cross section)
- straws, including flexi-straws
- different size and shaped balloons
- masking tape
- sharp pencil
- scissors
- ruler
- straight pins
- meterstick

Task Requirements

1. Research: A one- to two-page paper summarizing your research on Newton's Third Law of Motion and balloon-powered racers. Cite your sources. Your paper may include two pictures.
2. Model: A labeled drawing of the design of your racer and explanation of your strategy.
3. Results: A record, analysis, and interpretation of test results.
4. Conclusion: A summary of the task and what actually happened. It should include the purpose, a brief description of the test procedure, and explanation of results.
5. Reflection: Think about your team's choices for the design of your racer. Then complete the "Refection" handout.
6. Evaluation: Think about your behavior and performance as a team member. Then complete the "Self-Evaluation Rubric."

Egg-Drop Contraption

Task: Design a contraption that will keep a raw egg from cracking when dropped from 10 feet.

What You Should Know

The primary function of food packaging is to protect the product from damage during shipment and storage.

Steps to Follow

Work with a team to complete the steps listed below. A team will have 3 or 4 members.

Step 1:   Research Newton's Laws of Motion and product packaging.
Step 2:   Brainstorm ideas about how you might design a contraption that will keep a raw egg from cracking when dropped from a height of 10 feet.
Step 3:   Draw a diagram of your contraption.
Step 4:   Construct your contraption.
Step 5:   Test your contraption.
Step 6:   Evaluate the performance of your contraption.
Step 7:   Identify how to improve the design of your contraption.
Step 8:   Make the needed changes.
Step 9:   Retest and re-evaluate your contraption.
Step 10:   Share your results.

Terminology You Should Know

Newton's First Law of Motion: the law states that an object in motion stays in motion while an object at rest stays at rest unless being acted on by an outside force

Newton's Second Law of Motion: the law states that acceleration depends on the mass of an object and the force pushing or pulling the object

Newton's Third Law of Motion: the law states that for every action, there is an equal and opposite reaction

Materials You May Need

- 16 flex straws
- raw eggs
- meterstick
- two pieces of construction paper
- three paper clips
- one meter of string
- three rubber bands
- 10 craft sticks

Task Requirements

1. <u>Research</u>: A one- to two-page paper summarizing your research on Newton's Laws of Motion and product packaging. Cite your sources. Your paper may include two pictures.
2. <u>Model</u>: A labeled drawing of your contraption and explanation of your strategy.
3. <u>Results</u>: A record, analysis, and interpretation of test results.
4. <u>Conclusion</u>: A summary of the task and what actually happened. It should include the purpose, a brief description of the test procedure, and explanation of results.
5. <u>Reflection</u>: Think about your team's choices and the design of your contraption. Then complete the "Reflection" handout.
6. <u>Evaluation</u>: Think about your behavior and performance as a team member. Then complete the "Self-Evaluation Rubric."

Periscope

Task: Design a periscope to look around corners and over objects.

What You Should Know

A periscope is an instrument people use to look at things from a hidden position. It has a long tube with parallel mirrors positioned at both ends at a 45-degree angle. A submarine uses a periscope as a way to see above the surface while still underwater.

Steps to Follow

Work with a team to complete the steps listed below. A team will have 3 or 4 members.

Step 1: Research periscopes, mirrors, and reflection.
Step 2: Brainstorm ideas about how you might design and build a periscope.
Step 3: Draw a diagram of your periscope.
Step 4: Construct your periscope.
Step 5: Test your periscope.
Step 6: Evaluate the performance of your periscope.
Step 7: Identify how to improve the design of your periscope.
Step 8: Make the needed changes.
Step 9: Retest and re-evaluate your periscope design.
Step 10: Share your results.

Terminology You Should Know

light energy: the energy carried by light and other kinds of electromagnetic waves

plane mirror: a mirror with a flat reflective surface

reflection: the light energy bouncing off an object or surface

Materials You May Need

- large cereal box or large piece of cardboard
- masking or duct tape
- scissors
- glue
- small mirrors

Task Requirements

1. <u>Research</u>: A one- to two-page paper summarizing your research on periscopes, mirrors, and reflection. Cite your sources. Your paper may include two pictures.
2. <u>Model</u>: A labeled drawing of your periscope design and explanation of your strategy.
3. <u>Results</u>: A record, analysis, and interpretation of test results.
4. <u>Conclusion</u>: A summary of the task and what actually happened. It should include the purpose, a brief description of the test procedure, and explanation of results.
5. <u>Reflection</u>: Think about your team's choices and your periscope design. Then complete the "Reflection" handout.
6. <u>Evaluation</u>: Think about your behavior and performance as a team member. Then complete the "Self-Evaluation Rubric."

Kaleidoscope

Task: Design a kaleidoscope that will reflect light waves to create colorful patterns.

What You Should Know

A kaleidoscope uses mirrors to reflect light. The light waves reflect back and forth inside the kaleidoscope, allowing the creation of multiple images.

Steps to Follow

Work with a team to complete the steps listed below. A team will have 3 or 4 members.

Step 1:   Research light energy, mirrors, and kaleidoscopes.

Step 2:   Brainstorm ideas about how you might design a device that reflects light waves to create colorful patterns.

Step 3:   Draw a diagram of your kaleidoscope.

Step 4:   Construct your kaleidoscope.

Step 5:   Test your kaleidoscope.

Step 6:   Evaluate the performance of your kaleidoscope.

Step 7:   Identify how to improve the design of your kaleidoscope.

Step 8:   Make the needed changes.

Step 9:   Retest and re-evaluate your kaleidoscope.

Step 10: Share your results.

Terminology You Should Know

law of reflection: the law states that light will always be reflected by a surface at the same angle at which it hits the surface

light energy: the energy carried by light and other kinds of electromagnetic waves

mirror: a surface capable of reflecting sufficient undiffused light to form an image of an object placed in front of it

reflection: the light energy bouncing off an object or surface

translucent: a material that lets light pass through, but objects on the other side can't be seen clearly

white light: a combination of all the visible colors of the rainbow

Materials You May Need

- three identical-sized rectangular mirrors
- scissors
- construction paper
- hole punch
- tape
- old magazines

Task Requirements

1. Research: A one- to two-page paper summarizing your research on light energy, mirrors, and kaleidoscopes. Cite your sources. Your paper may include two pictures.
2. Model: A labeled drawing of your kaleidoscope design and explanation of your strategy.
3. Results: A record, analysis, and interpretation of test results.
4. Conclusion: A summary of the task and what actually happened. It should include the purpose, a brief description of the test procedure, and explanation of results.
5. Reflection: Think about your team's choices and kaleidoscope design. Then complete the "Reflection" handout.
6. Evaluation: Think about your behavior and performance as a team member. Then complete the "Self-Evaluation Rubric."

A Soundproof Box

Task: Design a soundproof box to keep the sounds of a clock's alarm contained.

What You Should Know

Noise is considered as any unwanted sound. Noise pollution can be harmful to your health. In the U.S., it is estimated that millions of people are exposed to unhealthy levels of noise, typically from automobiles, aircraft, traffic, and loud music.

Steps to Follow

Work with a team to complete the steps listed below. A team will have 3 or 4 members.

Step 1:   Research sound, noise pollution, and soundproofing.
Step 2:   Brainstorm ideas about how you might design a box to keep sound contained.
Step 3:   Draw a diagram of your soundproof box.
Step 4:   Construct your soundproof box.
Step 5:   Test your box.
Step 6:   Evaluate the performance of your box.
Step 7:   Identify how to improve the design of your soundproof box.
Step 8:   Make the needed changes.
Step 9:   Retest and re-evaluate your soundproof box.
Step 10: Share your results.

Terminology You Should Know

amplitude: the distance a wave oscillates from its resting position; increase amplitude, sound gets louder

frequency: the number of sound waves produced in a given time; the higher the frequency of the sound wave, the higher the pitch

sound energy: the energy carried by sound waves

Materials You May Need

- large cardboard box with lid
- shoe box with lid
- alarm clock
- soundproofing materials to be determined by students through their research

Task Requirements

1. <u>Research</u>: A one- to two-page paper summarizing your research on sound, noise pollution, and soundproofing. Cite your sources. Your paper may include two pictures.
2. <u>Model</u>: A labeled drawing of your soundproof box design and explanation of your strategy.
3. <u>Results</u>: A record, analysis, and interpretation of test results.
4. <u>Conclusion</u>: A summary of the task and what actually happened. It should include the purpose, a brief description of the test procedure, and explanation of results.
5. <u>Reflection</u>: Think about your team's choices and the design of your soundproof box. Then complete the "Reflection" handout.
6. <u>Evaluation</u>: Think about your behavior and performance as a team member. Then complete the "Self-Evaluation Rubric."

Stringed Instrument

Task: Design a stringed instrument to play a tune.

What You Should Know

A string instrument has strings in its body. The strings are either rubbed by a bow, plucked, or struck to produce different sounds, depending on the intensity of vibration produced.

Steps to Follow

Work with a team to complete the steps listed below. A team will have 3 or 4 members.

Step 1: Research sound energy, pitch, and stringed instruments.

Step 2: Brainstorm ideas about how you might design a model of a stringed instrument.

Step 3: Draw a diagram of your instrument.

Step 4: Construct your stringed instrument.

Step 5: Test your instrument.

Step 6: Evaluate the performance of your stringed instrument.

Step 7: Identify how to improve the design of your instrument.

Step 8: Make the needed changes.

Step 9: Retest and re-evaluate your instrument.

Step 10: Share your results.

Terminology You Should Know

decibel: a unit that measures the loudness of different sounds

frequency: the number of sound waves produced in a given time; the higher the frequency of the sound wave, the higher the pitch

hertz: the unit in which frequency is measured

pitch: the highness or lowness of sound, determined by the frequency of the wave

sound energy: the energy transferred by an object vibrating in the air

vibration: the repetition of back-and-forth or up-and-down motion

Materials You May Need

- sturdy shoe box with lid
- rubber bands of varying lengths and widths
- two pencils
- scissors
- duct tape
- craft sticks

Task Requirements

1. Research: A one- to two-page paper summarizing your research on sound energy, pitch, and stringed instruments. Cite your sources. Your paper may include two pictures.
2. Model: A labeled drawing of your instrument and explanation of your strategy.
3. Results: A record, analysis, and interpretation of test results.
4. Conclusion: A summary of the task and what actually happened. It should include the purpose, a brief description of the test procedure, and explanation of results.
5. Reflection: Think about your team's choices and your instrument design. Then complete the "Reflection" handout.
6. Evaluation: Think about your behavior and performance as a team member. Then complete the "Self-Evaluation Rubric."

Crystal Radio

Task: Design a simple crystal radio that can receive radio signals.

What You Should Know

The "golden age of radio" was in the 1930s and 1940s. Radios provided entertainment and news for most American households during this time. Since television wasn't available, people listened to, rather than viewed, programs like radio plays, adventure and detective serials, soap operas, and comedies, as well as live musical concerts and play-by-play sports broadcasts.

Steps to Follow

Work with a team to complete the steps listed below. A team will have 3 or 4 members.

Step 1: Research crystal radios, radio waves, and sound.
Step 2: Brainstorm ideas about how you might design a crystal radio.
Step 3: Draw a diagram of your radio.
Step 4: Construct your radio.
Step 5: Test your radio.
Step 6: Evaluate the performance of your radio.
Step 7: Identify how to improve your radio.
Step 8: Make the needed changes.
Step 9: Retest and re-evaluate your radio.
Step 10: Share your results.

Terminology You Should Know

crystal radio: a radio that only uses the power of the radio waves picked up by an antenna to generate sound heard in the head phones

germanium diode: a one-way conductor with two terminals, the positive and negative terminal

radio waves: a type of electromagnetic wave used for long-distance communication

sound energy: the energy carried by sound waves

Materials You May Need

- scissors
- sandpaper (coarse)
- sharp pencil
- wire strippers
- toilet paper tube
- two alligator clips
- germanium diode
- solid insulated wire
- crystal earphone (with wire leads)
- other materials determined through student research

Task Requirements

1. <u>Research</u>: A one- to two-page paper summarizing your research on crystal radios, radio waves, and sound. Cite your sources. Your paper may include two pictures.
2. <u>Model</u>: A labeled drawing of your radio design and explanation of your strategy.
3. <u>Results</u>: A record, analysis, and interpretation of test results.
4. <u>Conclusion</u>: A summary of the task and what actually happened. It should include the purpose, a brief description of the test procedure, and explanation of results.
5. <u>Reflection</u>: Think about your team's choices and your radio design. Then complete the "Reflection" handout.
6. <u>Evaluation</u>: Think about your behavior and performance as a team member. Then complete the "Self-Evaluation Rubric."

Low-Tech Ice-Cream Maker

Task: Design a low-tech ice-cream maker.

What You Should Know

Chemistry is behind making a great ice cream. Ice cream is a mixture where under normal circumstances the substances would separate from each other, but instead, they turn into a smooth frozen treat.

Steps to Follow

Work with a team to complete the steps listed below. A team will have 3 or 4 members.

Step 1: Research the chemistry behind ice-cream making.
Step 2: Brainstorm ideas about how you might design a low-tech ice-cream maker.
Step 3: Draw a diagram of your design.
Step 4: Construct your ice-cream maker.
Step 5: Test your ice-cream maker.
Step 6: Evaluate the performance of your ice-cream maker.
Step 7: Identify how to improve the design of your ice-cream maker.
Step 8: Make the needed changes in your ice-cream maker.
Step 9: Retest and re-evaluate your ice-cream maker.
Step 10: Share your results.

Terminology You Should Know

freezing point: the temperature at which a substance changes from a liquid to a solid

heat: the transfer of thermal energy between substances that are at different temperatures

mixture: two or more substances that are physically combined but not chemically joined together

states of matter: the different phases matter can take: solid, liquid, gas, and plasma

Materials You May Need

- various size metal or plastic coffee cans with lids
- rock salt
- crushed ice

Ice-Cream Recipe
- 1 cup milk
- 1 cup half-and-half
- $\frac{1}{4}$ cup sugar
- 1 teaspoon vanilla flavoring

Task Requirements

1. <u>Research</u>: A one- to two-page paper summarizing your research on the chemistry of ice-cream making. Cite your sources. Your paper may include two pictures.
2. <u>Model</u>: A labeled drawing of your ice-cream maker design and explanation of your strategy.
3. <u>Results</u>: A record, analysis, and interpretation of test results.
4. <u>Conclusion</u>: A summary of the task and what actually happened. It should include the purpose, a brief description of the test procedure, and explanation of results.
5. <u>Reflection</u>: Think about your team's choices and the design of your ice-cream maker. Then complete the "Reflection" handout.
6. <u>Evaluation</u>: Think about your behavior and performance as a team member. Then complete the "Self-Evaluation Rubric."

Plant and Animal Cells

Task: Design a three-dimensional model of a plant and an animal cell that will illustrate the similarities and differences of the two types of cells.

What You Should Know

All organisms are made up of cells. All cells have three things in common. They have a nucleus, cell membrane, and cytoplasm.

Materials You May Need

Materials to be determined by students through their research

Terminology You Should Know

cell membrane: the outside wall of a cell

cytoplasm: a gel-like material that contains proteins, nutrients, and all of the other cell organelles

nucleus: the control center for the cell

organelle: a tiny structure in the cytoplasm that does a specific job for the cell

Steps to Follow

Work with a team to complete the steps listed below. A team will have 3 or 4 members.

Step 1: Research plant and animal cell structures and investigate how the components of a cell operate as a system.

Step 2: Brainstorm ideas about how you might make a model of a plant and animal cell illustrating the similarities and differences.

Step 3: Draw a diagram of your two cell models.

Step 4: Construct your models.

Step 5: Test the accuracy of your models by using your science book or other resources. Record the results of your comparison.

Step 6: Evaluate your cell models. Identify items selected to represent the various cell structures and assess how well the items chosen represent the actual parts of the cells.

Step 7: Identify how to improve the design of your two cell models.

Step 8: Make the needed changes.

Step 9: Retest and re-evaluate the design of your two cell models.

Step 10: Share your results.

Task Requirements

1. Research: A one- to two-page paper summarizing your research on plant and animal cells. Cite your sources. Your paper may include two pictures.

2. Model: A labeled drawing of your plant and animal cell models and explanation of your strategy.

3. Results: A record, analysis, and interpretation of test results.

4. Conclusion: A summary of the task and what actually happened. It should include the purpose, a brief description of the test procedure, and explanation of results.

5. Reflection: Think about your team's choices and your cell model designs. Then complete the "Reflection" handout.

6. Evaluation: Think about your behavior and performance as a team member. Then complete the "Self-Evaluation Rubric."

Neurons

Task: Design a three-dimensional labeled model of a neuron to learn about its structure.

What You Should Know

The brain is made up of billions of nerve cells called neurons. Neurons are cells that send and receive electro-chemical signals to and from the brain and nervous system. A neuron has four basic parts: dendrites, soma, axon, and axon terminal.

Terminology You Should Know

nervous system: the system of nerve cells that transmits nerve impulses between parts of the body

neuron: a brain cell that sends and receives electro-chemical signals to and from the brain and nervous system

Materials You May Need

Materials to be determined by students through their research

Steps to Follow

Work with a team to complete the steps listed below. A team will have 3 or 4 members.

Step 1:   Research neuron cell structures and investigate how the components of a cell operate as a system.

Step 2:   Brainstorm ideas about how you might make a model of a neuron cell.

Step 3:   Draw a diagram of your neuron cell model.

Step 4:   Construct your model.

Step 5:   Test the accuracy of your model by using your science book or other resources. Record the results of your comparison.

Step 6:   Evaluate your neuron cell model. Identify items selected to represent the various cell structures and assess how well the items chosen represent the actual parts of the cell.

Step 7:   Identify how to improve the design of your neuron cell model.

Step 8:   Make the needed changes.

Step 9:   Retest and re-evaluate the design of your neuron cell model.

Step 10: Share your results.

Task Requirements

1. Research: A one- to two-page paper summarizing your research on neuron cell structures. Cite your sources. Your paper may include two pictures.
2. Model: A labeled drawing of your neuron cell model and explanation of your strategy.
3. Results: A record, analysis, and interpretation of test results.
4. Conclusion: A summary of the task and what actually happened. It should include the purpose, a brief description of the test procedure, and explanation of results.
5. Reflection: Think about your team's choices and your neuron cell model design. Then complete the "Reflection" handout.
6. Evaluation: Think about your behavior and performance as a team member. Then complete the "Self-Evaluation Rubric."

DNA

Task: Design a three-dimenisonal DNA model.

What You Should Know

A single DNA molecule, or ladder, can have thousands of rungs, or steps. The number of steps and how they are arranged form a genetic code. The genetic code determines the different kinds of inherited traits.

Materials You May Need

- different-colored beads
- pipe cleaners

Terminology You Should Know

chromosomes: the rod-shaped strands containing genetic material

DNA: the genetic blueprint (code) for how an organism looks and functions

gene: the small section of a chromosome that determines a trait

trait: a characteristic

Steps to Follow
Work with a team to complete the steps listed below. A team will have 3 or 4 members.

Step 1:   Research DNA structure.
Step 2:   Brainstorm ideas about how you might make a DNA model.
Step 3:   Draw a diagram of your model.
Step 4:   Construct your DNA model.
Step 5:   Test the accuracy of your model by using your science book or other resources. Record the results of your comparison.
Step 6:   Evaluate your DNA model. Identify items selected to represent the various cell structures and assess how well the items chosen represent the actual parts of the DNA model.
Step 7:   Identify how to improve the design of your model.
Step 8:   Make the needed changes.
Step 9:   Retest and re-evaluate the design of your DNA model.
Step 10:   Share your results.

Task Requirements

1. <u>Research</u>: A one- to two-page paper summarizing your research on DNA. Cite your sources. Your paper may include two pictures.
2. <u>Model</u>: A labeled drawing of your DNA model and explanation of your strategy.
3. <u>Results</u>: A record, analysis, and interpretation of test results.
4. <u>Conclusion</u>: A summary of the task and what actually happened. It should include the purpose, a brief description of the test procedure, and explanation of results.
5. <u>Reflection</u>: Think about your team's choices and your DNA model design. Then complete the "Reflection" handout.
6. <u>Evaluation</u>: Think about your behavior and performance as a team member. Then complete the "Self-Evaluation Rubric."

Egg Incubator

Task: Design an egg incubator that will hatch several chicken eggs within 22 days. (This task requires adult supervision.)

What You Should Know

The chicken is one of the most common and widespread domestic animals. People keep chickens primarily as a source of food. Once found mainly in rural areas on farms, coops filled with chickens are now becoming a common fixture in many urban and suburban backyards.

Steps to Follow

Work with a team to complete the steps listed below. A team will have 3 or 4 members.

Step 1:   Research chickens, hatching chicken eggs, egg incubators, and special care needed by baby chickens.

Step 2:   Brainstorm ideas for the design of your incubator. Consider how often eggs need to be turned a day and how to keep the correct temperature and humidity for incubating eggs.

Step 3:   Draw a diagram of your incubator.

Step 4:   Construct your incubator.

Step 5:   Test and evaluate the performance of your incubator.

Step 6:   Identify how to improve your design and make needed changes.

Step 7:   Retest and re-evaluate your design.

Step 8:   Share your results.

Terminology You Should Know

bird: a warm-blooded, egg-laying vertebrate with feathers, wings, and a beak, and usually able to fly

fertilization: a sperm cell unites with an egg cell

life cycle: the series of stages through which a living thing passes from the beginning of its life until its death

sexual reproduction: a process where a new cell is formed when DNA from both parents combine

vertebrate: an animal with a backbone

warm-blooded: an animal that maintains a constant body temperature

* Make sure you have located homes for all the chicks you may hatch.

Materials You May Need

- heavy cardboard box with lid
- several fertilized chicken eggs
- 60-watt light bulb
- light socket with plug-in cord
- thermometer   • hydrometer
- masking tape   • box
- small pan   • water

** Wash your hands with warm soapy water after handling the eggs or baby chicks.

Task Requirements

1. <u>Research</u>: A one- to two-page paper summarizing your research and citing your sources. Your paper may include two pictures.
2. <u>Model</u>: A labeled drawing of your incubator design and explanation of your strategy.
3. <u>Results</u>: A record, analysis, and interpretation of test results.
4. <u>Conclusions</u>: A summary of the task and what actually happened. It should include the purpose, a brief description of the test procedure, and explanation of results.
5. <u>Reflection</u>: Think about the design of your incubator. Then complete the "Reflection" handout.
6. <u>Evaluation</u>: Think about your behavior and performance as a team member. Then complete the "Self-Evaluation Rubric."

Birdhouse

Task: Design a bird house for a wild bird species in your area, and place it where birds can use it for nesting.

What You Should Know

Birdhouses or nest-boxes are used by birds that nest in cavities or holes in trees.

Steps to Follow

Work with a team to complete the steps listed below. A team will have 3 or 4 members.

Step 1:   Research wild birds in your area, where they build nests, what they eat, and their migration patterns.

Step 2:   Brainstorm ideas about how you might design a birdhouse. Consider that different kinds of birds need different-sized houses. Other important factors to consider are the diameter of the opening in the nest-box and placement dimensions of the floor.

Step 3:   Draw a diagram of your birdhouse.

Step 4:   Construct your birdhouse.

Step 5:   Test your birdhouse.

Step 6:   Evaluate your design.

Step 7:   Identify how to improve the design of your birdhouse.

Step 8:   Make the needed changes.

Step 9:   Retest and re-evaluate your birdhouse.

Step 10: Share your results.

Terminology You Should Know

bird: a warm-blooded, egg-laying vertebrate with feathers, wings, and a beak, and usually able to fly

ecosystem: the interaction of all living things and nonliving things in an environment

habitat: the place where a plant or animal naturally lives and grows

migration: the movement of animals from one place to another during different seasons

species: a group of animals or plants that are similar and can produce young animals or plants

Materials You Will Need

- Materials to be determined by students through their research

Task Requirements

1. Research: A one- to two-page paper summarizing your bird and birdhouse research. Cite your sources. Your paper may include two pictures.
2. Model: A labeled drawing of your birdhouse design and explanation of your strategy.
3. Results: A record, analysis, and interpretation of test results.
4. Conclusions: A summary of the task and what actually happened. It should include the purpose, a brief description of the test procedure, and explanation of results.
5. Reflection: Think about your team's choices and your birdhouse design. Then complete the "Refection" handout.
6. Evaluation: Think about your behavior and performance as a team member. Then complete the "Self-Evaluation Rubric."

Aqua Scope

Task: Design an aqua scope that will allow you to observe water life. With an adult supervisor, visit a freshwater biome. Use your aqua scope to discover the underwater world. Record your observations. (Alternatively, use your aqua scope to examine an artificial freshwater biome set up in your classroom.)

What You Should Know

There are three main types of freshwater biomes: ponds and lakes, streams and rivers, and wetlands. A variety of plants and animals can be found in and around each freshwater ecosystem.

Steps to Follow

Work with a team to complete the steps listed below. A team will have 3 or 4 members.

Step 1:   Research fresh water biomes and aqua scopes.
Step 2:   Brainstorm ideas about how you might design an aqua scope.
Step 3:   Draw a diagram of your aqua scope.
Step 4:   Construct your aqua scope.
Step 5:   Test your aqua scope.
Step 6:   Evaluate the performance of your aqua scope.
Step 7:   Identify how to improve the design of your aqua scope.
Step 8:   Make the needed changes.
Step 9:   Retest and re-evaluate your design.
Step 10: Share your results.

Terminology You Should Know

biome: a large ecosystem with its own kind of climate, soil, plants, and animals

ecosystem: the interaction of all living and nonliving things in an environment

habitat: the place where a plant or animal naturally lives and grows

niche: the role of an organism in a ecosystem

Materials You May Need

- various types and sizes of containers: plastic yogurt cartons, juice can, tin coffee can
- heavy clear plastic cap
- rubber bands
- X-acto knife (use with adult supervision)
- scissors
- can opener

Task Requirements

1. Research: A one- to two-page paper summarizing your research on freshwater biomes and aqua scopes. Cite your sources. Your paper may include two pictures.
2. Model: A labeled drawing of your aqua scope design and explanation of your strategy.
3. Results: A record, analysis, and interpretation of test results.
4. Conclusion: A summary of the task and what actually happened. It should include the purpose, a brief description of the test procedure, and explanation of results.
5. Reflection: Think about your team's choices and the design of your aqua scope. Then complete the "Reflection" handout.
6. Evaluation: Think about your behavior and performance as a team member. Then complete the "Self-Evaluation Rubric."

Camouflage

Task: Design a color pattern for a camouflage suit.

What You Should Know

Camouflage is an adaptation that helps animals survive. When animals are camouflaged, the body color blends into its surroundings thus making it difficult for their prey or their predators to see them.

Steps to Follow

Work with a team to complete the steps listed below. A team will have 3 or 4 members.

Step 1: Choose and research a biome. Research animal adaptations and camouflage.

Step 2: Brainstorm ideas about how you might design a color pattern for a camouflage suit. Consider animals that use camouflage in your biome.

Step 3: Draw a diagram of your camouflage pattern.

Step 4: Create the pattern.

Step 5: Test your pattern.

Step 6: Evaluate the performance of your pattern.

Step 7: Identify how to improve the pattern.

Step 8: Make the needed changes.

Step 9: Retest and re-revaluate your pattern.

Step 10: Share your results.

Terminology You Should Know

biome: a large ecosystem with its own kind of climate, soil, plants, and animals

coloration: an appearance that allows an animal to conceal itself in a background of the same color

disguise: the way an animal conceals itself by resembling another object

disruptive coloration: the stripes, spots, or pattern of the animal that allows it to appear relatively indistinguishable from others in a group

mimicry: an action that allows an animal to resemble an animal that is dangerous to predators

predator: an animal that hunts other animals for food

prey: a living thing that is hunted for food

Materials You May Need

- colored picture of your chosen biome
- coffee filters
- washable markers
- spray bottle with water (after completing the camouflage pattern, give it a mist of water to blur the edges and create a more natural effect)

Task Requirements

1. Research: A one- to two-page paper summarizing your research on biomes and animal camouflage. Cite your sources. Your paper may include two pictures.
2. Model: A labeled drawing of your pattern and explanation of your strategy.
3. Results: A record, analysis, and interpretation of test results.
4. Conclusion: A summary of the task and what actually happened. It should include the purpose, a brief description of the test procedure, and explanation of results.
5. Reflection: Think about your team's choices and the design of your camouflage pattern. Then complete the "Reflection" handout.
6. Evaluation: Think about your behavior and performance as a team member. Then complete the "Self-Evaluation Rubric."

Desert Shelter

Task: Design a human shelter to withstand the extreme desert conditions based on an animal's habitat.

What You Should Know

Deserts are dry and barren. Animals that live in these regions must be able to survive in these extreme environments.

Steps to Follow

Work with a team to complete the steps listed below. A team will have 3 or 4 members.

Step 1:   Research the desert biome. Choose an animal to research. Research ways in which the animal builds its shelter. Use the information to design your structure. Consider insulation and ventilation.

Step 2:   Brainstorm ideas about how you might design your structure using information from your research.

Step 3:   Draw a diagram of your structure.

Step 4:   Construct your structure.

Step 5:   Test your structure.

Step 6:   Evaluate your structure.

Step 7:   Identify how to improve the design of your structure.

Step 8:   Make the needed changes.

Step 9:   Retest and re-evaluate your structure.

Step 10: Share your results.

Terminology You Should Know

biome: a large ecosystem with its own kind of climate, soil, plants, and animals

climate: the average weather pattern of a region

desert: a barren area of land with very little precipitation

habitat: the place where a plant or animal naturally lives and grows

Materials You May Need

- thermometers
- timer
- heat lamp (use with adult supervision)
- sand
- design materials: to be determined by students through their research

Task Requirements

1. Research: A one- to two-page paper summarizing your research on the animal of your choice and the desert biome. Cite your sources. Your paper may include two pictures.
2. Model: A labeled drawing of your desert shelter design and explanation of your strategy.
3. Results: A record, analysis, and interpretation of test results.
4. Conclusion: A summary of the task and what actually happened. It should include the purpose, a brief description of the test procedure, and explanation of results.
5. Reflection: Think about your team's choices and the design of the structure. Then complete the "Reflection" handout.
6. Evaluation: Think about your behavior and performance as a team member. Then complete the "Self-Evaluation Rubric."

Desert Moisture Trap

Task: Design a moisture trap that catches water as the temperature drops.

What You Should Know

Deserts receive less than 10 inches of precipitation a year. They are hot and dry during the day and cold at night. The dry, hot temperatures can make you dehydrate quickly. For people lost in the desert, a small drink of water could mean the difference between life and death.

Steps to Follow

Work with a team to complete the steps listed below. A team will have 3 or 4 members.

Step 1: Research moisture traps and desert biomes.

Step 2: Brainstorm ideas about how to make a moisture trap. Consider how the diameter of the trap might affect the amount of water collected.

Step 3: Draw a diagram of your trap.

Step 4: Construct your moisture trap.

Step 5: Test your trap.

Step 6: Evaluate the performance of your trap.

Step 7: Identify how to improve your moisture trap design.

Step 8: Make the needed changes.

Step 9: Retest and re-evaluate your trap design.

Step 10: Share your results.

Terminology You Should Know

biome: a large ecosystem with its own kind of climate, soil, plants, and animals

condensation: the process in which matter changes from a gaseous state to a liquid state

evaporation: the process in which liquid water changes into invisible water vapor

temperature: a measure of the warmth or coldness of an object or substance with reference to some standard value

water vapor: the gaseous state of water

Materials You May Need

- shovel (use with supervision)
- small pebbles
- large rocks
- plastic sheeting
- plastic container

* Note: Don't drink any of the water that you collect in the moisture trap. It has not been sterilized and is not safe to drink.

Task Requirements

1. Research: A one- to two-page paper summarizing your research on moisture traps and desert biomes. Cite your sources. Your paper may include two pictures.
2. Model: A labeled drawing of your trap design and explanation of your strategy.
3. Results: A record, analysis, and interpretation of test results.
4. Conclusion: A summary of the task and what actually happened. It should include the purpose, a brief description of the test procedure, and explanation of results.
5. Reflection: Think about your team's choices and your moisture trap design. Then complete the "Reflection" handout.
6. Evaluation: Think about your behavior and performance as a team member. Then complete the "Self-Evaluation Rubric."

Human Arm Model

Task: Design a human arm model that will pick up a paper cup.

What You Should Know

The human arm is a complex structure made up of bones, joints, ligaments, and muscles. A robotic arm is a type of mechanical arm, usually programmable, with similar functions to a human arm. A human arm model simulates the muscles and motion of an actual human arm.

Steps to Follow

Work with a team to complete the steps listed below. A team will have 3 or 4 members.

Step 1: Research the human arm, robotic arms, and human arm models.
Step 2: Brainstorm ideas about how you might design a human arm model.
Step 3: Draw a diagram of your model.
Step 4: Construct a model of your human arm that can pick up a cup.
Step 5: Test your arm model.
Step 6: Evaluate the performance of your model.
Step 7: Identify how to improve the design of your human arm model.
Step 8: Make the needed changes.
Step 9: Retest and re-evaluate your arm design.
Step 10: Share your results.

Terminology You Should Know

compression: a pushing, squeezing force

friction: a force that resists motion

fulcrum: the point around which a lever turns

lever: a rigid bar that is free to rotate about a point called a fulcrum

tension: a pulling, stretching force

Materials You May Need

- corrugated cardboard
- hole punch
- tape
- two large paper clips
- paper cups (3 oz.)
- drinking straw
- one inch brass fastener
- fishing line

Task Requirements

1. Research: A one- to two-page paper summarizing your research on human and robotic arms. Cite your sources. Your paper may include two pictures.
2. Model: A labeled drawing of your human arm model and explanation of your strategy.
3. Results: A record, analysis, and interpretation of test results.
4. Conclusions: A summary of the task and what actually happened. It should include the purpose, a brief description of the test procedure, and explanation of results.
5. Reflection: Think about your team's choice and your human arm model design. Then complete the "Refection" handout.
6. Evaluation: Think about your behavior and performance as a team member. Then complete the "Self-Evaluation Rubric."

Wind Direction Recorder

Task: Design a wind recorder to measure the direction from which the wind blows.

What You Should Know

When a weather forecaster says "a north wind," that person is referring to the direction the wind is blowing from, not where it is blowing to.

Steps to Follow

Work with a team to complete the steps listed below. A team will have 3 or 4 members.

Step 1:   Research weather, wind, global winds, and jet stream.
Step 2:   Brainstorm ideas for the design of your wind recorder.
Step 3:   Draw a diagram of your recorder.
Step 4:   Construct your wind recorder.
Step 5:   Test your wind recorder.
Step 6:   Evaluate the performance of your wind recorder.
Step 7:   Identify how to improve the design of your wind recorder.
Step 8:   Make the needed changes.
Step 9:   Retest and re-evaluate your wind recorder design.
Step 10: Share your results.

Terminology You Should Know

weather: the condition of the lower atmosphere from day to day at any given place and time; heat, dryness, sunshine, wind, rain, etc.

wind: the natural movement of air

Materials You May Need

- shoe box with lid
- several wooden thread spools
- different length dowel rods to fit in spool opening
- strong cardboard
- large stone
- compass
- scissors
- pencil
- paper
- glue
- tape

Task Requirements

1. Research: A one- to two-page paper summarizing your research on weather, wind, global winds, and jet stream. Cite your sources. Your paper may include two pictures.
2. Model: A labeled drawing of your wind recorder design and explanation of your strategy.
3. Results: A record, analysis, and interpretation of test results.
4. Conclusions: A summary of the task and what actually happened. It should include the purpose, a brief description of the test procedure, and explanation of results.
5. Reflection: Think about the design of your wind recorder. Then complete the "Reflection" handout.
6. Evaluation: Think about your behavior and performance as a team member. Then complete the "Self-Evaluation Rubric."

Psychrometer

Task: Design a psychrometer that will measure the level of humidity in the air.

What You Should Know

Weather forecasters use humidity to indicate the likelihood of precipitation, dew, or fog. Humidity can make a warm day feel warmer and a cool day feel cold. In high humidity, the air may feel "sticky" or "muggy," and perspiration will not evaporate easily because the air already contains so much water vapor.

Steps to Follow

Work with a team to complete the steps listed below. A team will have 3 or 4 members.

Step 1:   Research humidity, relative humidity, and psychrometers.

Step 2:   Brainstorm ideas about how you might design your psychrometer.

Step 3:   Draw a diagram of your device.

Step 4:   Construct your psychrometer.

Step 5:   Test and evaluate the performance of your psychrometer.

Step 6:   Identify how to improve your psychrometer design.

Step 7:   Make needed changes.

Step 8:   Retest and re-evaluate your psychrometer design.

Step 9:   Share your results.

Terminology You Should Know

dew point: the air temperature at which dew will form under certain conditions

evaporation: the process in which liquid water changes into invisible water vapor

humidity: the measure of the amount of water vapor in a given mass of air

psychrometer: an instrument used to measure the relative humidity of the air

relative humidity: the amount of water an air mass is holding relative to the maximum amount it could hold when completely saturated

Materials You May Need

- two thermometers
- gauze
- tape
- rubber band
- glass jar
- water

Task Requirements

1. <u>Research</u>: A one- to two-page paper summarizing your research on humidity, relative humidity, and psychrometers. Cite your sources. Your paper may include two pictures.
2. <u>Model</u>: A labeled drawing of your psychrometer and explanation of your strategy.
3. <u>Results</u>: A record, analysis, and interpretation of test results.
4. <u>Conclusion</u>: A summary of the task and what actually happened. It should include the purpose, a brief description of the test procedure, and explanation of results.
5. <u>Reflection</u>: Think about your team's choices and your psychrometer design. Then complete the "Reflection" handout.
6. <u>Evaluation</u>: Think about your behavior and performance as a team member. Then complete the "Self-Evaluation Rubric."

Seismograph

Task: Design a seismograph that can be used to measure seismic waves generated by an earthquake.

What You Should Know

While earthquakes can be very destructive and cause a great deal of damage and loss of life, many are so minor that they go unnoticed by most people. In order to discover the force of a particular earthquake, seismologists use an instrument called a seismograph.

Steps to Follow

Work with a team to complete the steps listed below. A team will have 3 or 4 members.

Step 1:   Research earthquakes and seismographs.
Step 2:   Brainstorm ideas for the design of your seismograph.
Step 3:   Draw a diagram of your seismograph.
Step 4:   Construct your seismograph.
Step 5:   Test your seismograph.
Step 6:   Evaluate the performance of your seismograph.
Step 7:   Identify how to improve your design.
Step 8:   Make the needed changes.
Step 9:   Retest and re-evaluate your design.
Step 10: Share your results.

Terminology You Should Know

earthquake: the movement of the earth's surface caused by waves of energy released as rocks move along faults in the crust or volcanic activity inside the earth

epicenter: the spot on the earth's surface that is above the focus of an earthquake

pendulum: a weight hung from a fixed point so that it can swing freely backward and forward

seismograph: an instrument used to measure the motions of the earth's surface

Materials You May Need

- various size cereal boxes
- masking tape and duct tape
- paper
- paper cups with lids
- pens and pencils
- string
- rubber bands
- scissors
- sand

Task Requirements

1. <u>Research</u>: A one- to two-page paper summarizing your research on earthquakes and seismographs. Cite your sources. Your paper may include two pictures.
2. <u>Model</u>: A labeled drawing of your design and explanation of your strategy.
3. <u>Results</u>: A record, analysis, and interpretation of test results.
4. <u>Conclusions</u>: A summary of the task and what actually happened. It should include the purpose, a brief description of the test procedure, and explanation of results.
5. <u>Reflection</u>: Think about the design of your seismograph. Then complete the "Reflection" handout.
6. <u>Evaluation</u>: Think about your behavior and performance as a team member. Then complete the "Self-Evaluation Rubric."

Desalination

Task: Design a system that could be used to produce fresh water from salt water.

What You Should Know

Fresh water is a natural resource. About three-fourths of Earth is covered in water, but only a small fraction of it is fresh water.

Steps to Follow

Work with a team to complete the steps listed below. A team will have 3 or 4 members.

Step 1:   Research the water cycle and desalination.
Step 2:   Brainstorm ideas about how you might design a system that would make fresh water from salt water.
Step 3:   Draw a diagram of your system.
Step 4:   Construct your system.
Step 5:   Test your system.
Step 6:   Evaluate the performance of your system.
Step 7:   Identify how to improve your system for producing fresh water from salt water.
Step 8:   Make the needed changes.
Step 9:   Retest and re-evaluate your system.
Step 10: Share your results.

Terminology You Should Know

desalination: a process that removes minerals from saline water

saline water: a liquid mixture of salt and water

sodium chloride (NaCl): a compound formed by sodium and chloride; salt

water cycle: a cycle in which water moves through the environment, through the processes of evaporation, condensation, and precipitation

Materials You May Need

- glass aquarium
- drinking glass
- paper cup
- salt water
- clear plastic food wrap
- masking tape
- ice cubes
- sunlight

Task Requirements

1. <u>Research</u>: A one- to two-page paper summarizing your research on desalination and the water cycle. Cite your sources. Your paper may include two pictures.
2. <u>Model</u>: A labeled drawing of your desalination system and explanation of your strategy.
3. <u>Results</u>: A record, analysis, and interpretation of test results.
4. <u>Conclusion</u>: A summary of the task and what actually happened. It should include the purpose, a brief description of the test procedure, and explanation of results.
5. <u>Reflection</u>: Think about your team's choices and the design of your desalination system. Then complete the "Reflection" handout.
6. <u>Evaluation</u>: Think about your behavior and performance as a team member. Then complete the "Self-Evaluation Rubric."

Ancient Time-Keeping Device

Task: Design a sundial and take measurements to determine solar noon.

What You Should Know

Time can be measured by following the regular pattern of shadows cast by the sun's apparent motion across the sky.

Steps to Follow

Work with a team to complete the steps listed below. A team will have 3 or 4 members.

Step 1: Research the sun and sundials.
Step 2: Brainstorm ideas for the design of your sundial.
Step 3: Draw a diagram of your sundial.
Step 4: Construct your sundial.
Step 5: Test your sundial.
Step 6: Evaluate the performance of your sundial.
Step 7: Identify how to improve your sundial design.
Step 8: Make the needed changes.
Step 9: Retest and re-evaluate your sundial design.
Step 10: Share your results.

Terminology You Should Know

gnomon: an object that by the position or length of its shadow serves as an indicator, especially of the hour of the day

rotation: the spinning motion of the earth; it takes 23 hours and 56 minutes for the earth to complete one rotation

solar noon: the time when the sun is highest in the sky for any given day; it may not coincide with the noon on your watch

sun: the star at the center of our solar system

sundial: a device that tells the time of day by the apparent position of the sun in the sky

Materials You May Need

- compass
- cardboard
- blank paper
- plastic straw
- protractor
- tape
- clay
- dowel rod

Task Requirements

1. Research: A one- to two-page paper summarizing your research on the sun and sundials. Cite your sources. Your paper may include two pictures.
2. Model: A labeled drawing of your sundial design and explanation of your strategy.
3. Results: A record, analysis, and interpretation of test results.
4. Conclusions: A summary of the task and what actually happened. It should include the purpose, a brief description of the test procedure, and explanation of results.
5. Reflection: Think about the design of your sundial. Then complete the "Reflection" handout.
6. Evaluation: Think about your behavior and performance as a team member. Then complete the "Self-Evaluation Rubric."

Rocket Lift

Task: Construct a balloon-powered rocket to launch the greatest payload possible to the classroom ceiling.

What You Should Know

Rockets come in many sizes. Some rockets are more powerful than others. Different rockets have different purposes. A heavy lift rocket is the most powerful type of rocket and can do things that other rockets can't do.

Steps to Follow

Work with a team to complete the steps listed below. A team will have 3 or 4 members.

Step 1:   Research rockets, heavy lift rockets, and Newton's Third Law of Motion.

Step 2:   Brainstorm ideas about how you might design your rocket.

Step 3:   Draw a diagram of your rocket.

Step 4:   Construct your rocket.

Step 5:   Test your rocket.

Step 6:   Evaluate the performance of your rocket.

Step 7:   Identify how to improve the design of your rocket.

Step 8:   Make the needed changes.

Step 9:   Retest and re-evaluate your rocket design.

Step 10: Share your results.

Terminology You Should Know

Newton's Third Law of Motion: the law states that for every action, there is an equal and opposite reaction

thrust: the force that moves a rocket through air and space

Materials You May Need

- variety of sizes and shapes of balloons
- straws
- fishing line
- masking tape
- cups (3 oz. bathroom size)
- small baggies
- box of small paper clips
- clothes pins
- triple-beam balance

Task Requirements

1. <u>Research</u>: A one- to two-page paper summarizing your research on rockets, heavy lift rockets, and Newton's Third Law of Motion. Cite your sources. Your paper may include two pictures.
2. <u>Model</u>: A labeled drawing of your rocket design and explanation of your strategy.
3. <u>Results</u>: A record, analysis, and interpretation of test results.
4. <u>Conclusion</u>: A summary of the task and what actually happened. It should include the purpose, a brief description of the test procedure, and explanation of results.
5. <u>Reflection</u>: Think about your team's choices and your rocket design. Then complete the "Reflection" handout.
6. <u>Evaluation</u>: Think about your behavior and performance as a team member. Then complete the "Self-Evaluation Rubric."

Comets

Task: Create a model of a comet and simulate its orbit around the sun (light bulb) in a darkened room.

What You Should Know

A comet is often referred to as a "dirty snowball." Like other objects in our solar system, comets follow an orbit around the sun.

Steps to Follow

Work with a team to complete the steps listed below. A team will have 3 or 4 members.

Step 1: Research comets.
Step 2: Brainstorm ideas for creating a model of a comet. The material used in the construction of your comet must reflect the composition of real comets.
Step 3: Draw a diagram of your comet's path around the sun.
Step 4: Construct a model of your comet.
Step 5: Test and evaluate the performance of your comet.
Step 6: Identify how to improve your comet.
Step 7: Make the needed changes.
Step 8: Retest and re-evaluate your design.
Step 9: Share your results.

Terminology You Should Know

comet: a combination of ice, dust, and rock material that moves in an orbit around the sun

orbit: the path the moon, planets, asteroids, and comets follow as they travel around the sun

solar system: a star and all the objects that travel in orbit around it

Materials You Will Need

- Materials to be determined by students through their research

Task Requirements

1. <u>Research</u>: A one- to two-page paper summarizing your research on comets and citing your sources. Your paper may include two pictures.
2. <u>Model</u>: A labeled drawing of your comet model and explanation of your strategy.
3. <u>Results</u>: A record, analysis, and interpretation of test results.
4. <u>Conclusions</u>: A summary of the task and what actually happened. It should include the purpose, a brief description of the test procedure, and explanation of results.
5. <u>Reflection</u>: Think about the composition and the model of your comet. Then complete the "Reflection" handout.
6. <u>Evaluation</u>: Think about your behavior and performance as a team member. Then complete the "Self-Evaluation Rubric."

Sextant

Task: Design a sextant and measure the height (altitude) of a celestial object above the horizon.

What You Should Know

A sextant is an instrument that measures the angular altitude of a star above the horizon for the purpose of celestial navigation. The angle, and the time when it was measured, can be used to calculate a position line on a nautical or aeronautical chart.

Steps to Follow

Work with a team to complete the steps listed below. A team will have 3 or 4 members.

Step 1:   Research sextants and nautical and aeronautical navigation.

Step 2:   Brainstorm ideas about how you might design a sextant.

Step 3:   Draw a diagram of your sextant.

Step 4:   Construct your sextant.

Step 5:   Test your sextant.

Step 6:   Evaluate the performance of your sextant.

Step 7:   Identify how to improve the design of your sextant.

Step 8:   Make the needed changes.

Step 9:   Retest and re-evaluate your sextant design.

Step 10:   Share your results.

Terminology You Should Know

altitude: the height of an object in relation to sea level or ground level

celestial object: a natural object outside of Earth's atmosphere, such as the sun, moon, planets, stars, or an asteroid

horizon: the apparent line that separates the earth from the sky

plumb bob: a weight that is suspended from a string and used as a vertical reference line

zenith angle: the angle between the sun and the vertical; it is measured from the vertical rather than from the horizontal, thus making the zenith angle equal to 90° altitude

Materials You May Need

- wooden ruler
- tape
- string
- protractor
- steel washer
- compass

Task Requirements

1. <u>Research</u>: A one- to two-page paper summarizing your research on sextants and nautical and aeronautical navigation. Cite your sources. Your paper may include two pictures.
2. <u>Model</u>: A labeled drawing of your sextant design and explanation of your strategy.
3. <u>Results</u>: A record, analysis, and interpretation of test results.
4. <u>Conclusion</u>: A summary of the task and what actually happened. It should include the purpose, a brief description of the test procedure, and explanation of results.
5. <u>Reflection</u>: Think about your team's choices and your sextant design. Then complete the "Reflection" handout.
6. <u>Evaluation</u>: Think about your behavior and performance as a team member. Then complete the "Self-Evaluation Rubric."

Solar Oven

Task: Design a solar oven that will bake s'mores.

What You Should Know

Millions of people around the world cook over fires fueled by wood. However, in many places, wood is a scare resource. Solar energy is a simple and convenient alternative.

Steps to Follow

Work with a team to complete the steps listed below. A team will have 3 or 4 members.

Step 1: Research solar energy and solar ovens.

Step 2: Brainstorm ideas about how you might design a solar oven.

Step 3: Draw a diagram of your solar oven.

Step 4: Construct your solar oven.

Step 5: Test your solar oven.

Step 6: Evaluate the performance of your solar oven.

Step 7: Identify how to improve the design of your solar oven.

Step 8: Make the needed changes.

Step 9: Retest and re-evaluate your solar oven design.

Step 10: Share your results.

Terminology You Should Know

electromagnetic waves: a form of energy that can travel through empty space as well as water

heat: the transfer of thermal energy between substances that are at different temperatures

solar energy: the energy from the sun's rays that reach Earth

Materials You May Need

- warm, sunny day (85°F or hotter)
- various size pizza boxes
- pencil or pen
- ruler
- utility knife (use with adult supervision)
- scissors
- aluminum foil
- glue
- plastic wrap
- tape
- an assortment of colored paper
- wooden skewers
- graham crackers
- marshmallows
- chocolate bar

Task Requirements

1. <u>Research</u>: A one- to two-page paper summarizing your research on solar energy and solar ovens. Cite your sources. Your paper may include two pictures.
2. <u>Model</u>: A labeled drawing of your solar oven design and explanation of your strategy.
3. <u>Results</u>: A record, analysis, and interpretation of test results.
4. <u>Conclusion</u>: A summary of the task and what actually happened. It should include the purpose, a brief description of the test procedure, and explanation of results.
5. <u>Reflection</u>: Think about your team's choices and the design of your solar oven. Then complete the "Reflection" handout.
6. <u>Evaluation</u>: Think about your behavior and performance as a team member. Then complete the "Self-Evaluation Rubric."

Passive Solar Water Heater

Task: Design a passive solar water heater that will raise the temperature of tap water by 15°C in 15 minutes.

What You Should Know

The sun produces more energy in 60 minutes than the entire population of the world can use in one year.

Steps to Follow

Work with a team to complete the steps listed below. A team will have 3 or 4 members.

Step 1: Research passive solar water heaters.

Step 2: Brainstorm ideas for the design of your solar water heater.

Step 3: Draw a diagram of your solar water heater.

Step 4: Construct a model of your solar water heater.

Step 5: Test your solar water heater.

Step 6: Evaluate the performance of your solar water heater.

Step 7: Identify how to improve your design.

Step 8: Make the needed changes.

Step 9: Retest and re-evaluate your design.

Step 10: Share your results.

Terminology You Should Know

passive solar water heater: a system that takes solar thermal energy and transforms it to hot water without using any other form of energy

solar collector: a device that allows the sun's rays to heat water or other liquid

solar energy: the energy from the sun's rays that reach Earth

thermal energy: the energy that is generated and measured by heat

Materials You May Need

- clothespins
- plastic wrap
- timer
- tap water
- shoe box
- metric ruler
- plastic containers
- Celsius thermometer
- color plastic tubing or hose: clear, black, white, and green

Task Requirements

1. <u>Research</u>: A one- to two-page paper summarizing your research on passive solar water heaters. Cite your sources. Your paper may include two pictures.
2. <u>Model</u>: A labeled drawing of your passive solar water heater design and explanation of your strategy.
3. <u>Results</u>: A record, analysis, and interpretation of test results.
4. <u>Conclusions</u>: A summary of the task and what actually happened. It should include the purpose, a brief description of the test procedure, and explanation of results.
5. <u>Reflection</u>: Think about your team's choices and the design of your passive solar water heater. Then complete the "Reflection" handout.
6. <u>Evaluation</u>: Think about your behavior and performance as a team member. Then complete the "Self-Evaluation Rubric."

Photovoltaic Cell Racer

Task: Design a solar-powered racer that will travel straight to win a race.

What You Should Know

Solar-powered transportation is being developed as an alternative to fossil-fueled transportation. Scientists and engineers are looking at ways to make solar power an efficient and economical way to fuel cars, bicycles, and airplanes.

Steps to Follow

Work with a team to complete the steps listed below. A team will have 3 or 4 members.

Step 1: Research solar-powered racers, energy, solar energy, and photovoltaic cells.
Step 2: Brainstorm ideas about how you might design a solar racer. Consider the angle of the solar panel and time of day to race.
Step 3: Draw a diagram of your racer.
Step 4: Construct your racer.
Step 5: Test your racer.
Step 6: Evaluate the performance of your racer.
Step 7: Identify how to improve the design of your racer.
Step 8: Make the needed changes.
Step 9: Retest and re-evaluate your racer.
Step 10: Share your results.

Terminology You Should Know

chassis: the body of a motor vehicle

energy: a source of usable power

motor: a device that converts electrical or other energy into mechanical energy

photovoltaic cell (solar cell): a device that converts light directly into electricity

wheel-and-axle: a wheel attached to an axle so that these two parts rotate

Materials You May Need

- two solar cells with wires and motor pulley
- balsa wood sheets, cardboard, or similar materials
- water-bottle caps
- wire hanger or similar piece of hard, straight wire   • sunlight
- plastic straws   • elastic bands
- tape, glue, and hot glue gun
- various tools: pliers, scissors, screwdriver, ruler, pen or pencil
- other miscellaneous construction materials

Task Requirements

1. <u>Research</u>: A one- to two-page paper summarizing your research on solar-powered racers, energy, solar energy, and photovoltaic cells. Cite your sources. Your paper may include two pictures.
2. <u>Model</u>: A labeled drawing of your solar racer design and explanation of your strategy.
3. <u>Results</u>: A record, analysis, and interpretation of test results.
4. <u>Conclusion</u>: A summary of the task and what actually happened. It should include the purpose, a brief description of the test procedure, and explanation of results.
5. <u>Reflection</u>: Think about your team's choices and the design of your solar-powered racer. Then complete the "Reflection" handout.
6. <u>Evaluation</u>: Think about your behavior and performance as a team member. Then complete the "Self-Evaluation Rubric."

Windmill

Task: Design and construct a windmill that will convert wind energy into mechanical energy. The blades of the windmill must be able to rotate, causing a small object to be lifted upward.

What You Should Know

Wind is a renewable energy source that can be used to generate or supplement energy for homes and businesses. Windmills are machines that use a wheel-and-axle and vanes called sails or blades to convert energy from the wind into mechanical energy to do useful work.

Steps to Follow

Work with a team to complete the steps listed below. A team will have 3 or 4 members.

Step 1:   Research wind energy and windmills.
Step 2:   Brainstorm ideas about how you might design your windmill.
Step 3:   Draw a diagram of your windmill.
Step 4:   Construct your windmill.
Step 5:   Test the performance of your windmill.
Step 6:   Evaluate your windmill.
Step 7:   Identify how to improve your design.
Step 8:   Make the needed changes.
Step 9:   Retest and re-evaluate your windmill design.
Step 10:   Share your results.

Terminology You Should Know

energy: a source of usable power

mechanical energy: the energy an object has because of its motion or position; two kinds: kinetic and potential

renewable energy source: an energy source that is not limited and can be replaced by natural processes

wheel-and-axle: a wheel attached to an axle so that these two parts rotate

Materials You Will Need

- construction paper
- cardstock
- printer paper
- plastic straws
- string
- paper clip
- tape
- scissors
- glue
- wooden skewers
- hole punch

Task Requirements

1. <u>Research</u>: A one- to two-page paper summarizing your research on wind energy and windmills. Cite your sources. Your paper may include two pictures.
2. <u>Model</u>: A labeled drawing of your windmill design and explanation of your strategy.
3. <u>Results</u>: A record, analysis, and interpretation of test results.
4. <u>Conclusion</u>: A summary of the task and what actually happened. It should include the purpose, a brief description of the test procedure, and explanation of results.
5. <u>Reflection</u>: Think about your team's choices and your windmill design. Then complete the "Reflection" handout.
6. <u>Evaluation</u>: Think about your behavior and performance as a team member. Then complete the "Self-Evaluation Rubric."

Air-Cushion Vehicle

Task: Design an air-cushion vehicle that will carry one person across a tiled floor.

What You Should Know

An air-cushion vehicle (ACV) or hovercraft can carry passengers, vehicles, and freight. Some ACV's can travel as fast as 80 miles per hour.

Steps to Follow

Work with a team to complete the steps listed below. A team will have 3 or 4 members.

Step 1: Research Newton's Third Law of Motion, air-cushion vehicles, and hovercrafts.

Step 2: Brainstorm ideas about how you might design an ACV to carry one person. Consider placement and number of holes to be cut in the heavy plastic used to cover the bottom of the vehicle.

Step 3: Draw a diagram of your vehicle.

Step 4: Construct your vehicle.

Step 5: Test your vehicle.

Step 6: Evaluate the performance of your vehicle.

Step 7: Identify how to improve the design of your vehicle.

Step 8: Make the needed changes.

Step 9: Retest and re-evaluate your vehicle.

Step 10: Share your results.

Terminology You Should Know

air-cushion vehicle: a vehicle that travels on a layer of compressed air just above any kind of surface—land or water

friction: a force that resists motion

Newton's Third Law of Motion: the law states that for every action there is an equal and opposite reaction

Materials You May Need

- large Shop-Vac motor with reverse switch
- 100-ft extension cord
- staple gun and staples
- open, tiled floor
- duct tape
- electric drill
- plastic lid from a coffee can
- 4 ft. circle cut from $\frac{3}{4}$-inch thick plywood
- various size bolts, nuts, and washers
- a sheet of heavy plastic, larger than the plywood circle

Task Requirements

1. <u>Research</u>: A one- to two-page paper summarizing your research on Newton's Third Law of Motion, air-cushion vehicles, and hovercrafts. Cite your sources. Your paper may include two pictures.
2. <u>Model</u>: A labeled drawing of your ACV design and explanation of your strategy.
3. <u>Results</u>: A record, analysis, and interpretation of test results.
4. <u>Conclusion</u>: A summary of the task and what actually happened. It should include the purpose, a brief description of the test procedure, and explanation of results.
5. <u>Reflection</u>: Think about your team's choices and the design of your air-cushion vehicle. Then complete the "Reflection" handout.
6. <u>Evaluation</u>: Think about your behavior and performance as a team member. Then complete the "Self-Evaluation Rubric."

Hydro-Powered Turbine

Task: Design a small-scale water turbine that will lift a weight when water is fed through it.

What You Should Know

Hydroelectricity, also known as hydropower, is a renewable energy resource that can be harnessed to produce electricity. Water is stored in reservoirs behind dams built on rivers and lakes. Releasing the stored water causes turbines (giant wheels) at the base of the dam to turn. This spins a generator that converts the moving water into electricity.

Steps to Follow

Work with a team to complete the steps listed below. A team will have 3 or 4 members.

Step 1:   Research hydroelectricity and water turbines.
Step 2:   Brainstorm ideas about how to design your water turbine.
Step 3:   Draw a diagram of your turbine.
Step 4:   Construct your water turbine.
Step 5:   Test your turbine.
Step 6:   Evaluate the performance of your turbine.
Step 7:   Identify how to improve the design of your turbine.
Step 8:   Make the needed changes.
Step 9:   Retest and re-evaluate your design.
Step 10: Share your results.

Terminology You Should Know

electricity: the flow of electrical charges

hydropower: the power that can be harnessed from the energy of falling water or fast running water

kinetic energy: the energy an object has because it is in motion

mechanical energy: the energy an object has because of its motion or position

potential energy: the stored energy an object has because of its position, rather than its motion

Materials You May Need

- two-liter plastic soda bottle
- craft knife (use with adult supervision)
- scissors
- two corks
- barbeque skewer
- thread or string
- small objects to lift (small washer or sinker)
- duct tape
- funnel
- paper clips

Task Requirements

1. Research: A one- to two-page paper summarizing your research on hydroelectricity and water turbines. Cite your sources. Your paper may include two pictures.
2. Model: A labeled drawing of your turbine design and explanation of your strategy.
3. Results: A record, analysis, and interpretation of test results.
4. Conclusion: A summary of the task and what actually happened. It should include the purpose, a brief description of the test procedure, and explanation of results.
5. Reflection: Think about your team's choices and your turbine design. Then complete the "Reflection" handout.
6. Evaluation: Think about your behavior and performance as a team member. Then complete the "Self-Evaluation Rubric."

Hydrogen Fuel Cell

Task: Construct a hydrogen fuel cell that produces electricity.

What You Should Know

A hydrogen fuel cell combines hydrogen and oxygen to produce electricity, heat, and water without any pollution. Water is the only byproduct. Fuel cells are like batteries. Both convert the energy produced by a chemical reaction into usable electric power.

Steps to Follow

Work with a team to complete the steps listed below. A team will have 3 or 4 members.

Step 1:   Research fuel cells and hydrogen fuel cells.
Step 2:   Brainstorm ideas about how you might design a hydrogen fuel cell.
Step 3:   Draw a diagram of your fuel cell.
Step 4:   Construct your hydrogen fuel cell.
Step 5:   Test your hydrogen fuel cell.
Step 6:   Evaluate performance of your hydrogen fuel cell.
Step 7:   Identify how to improve the design of your hydrogen fuel cell.
Step 8:   Make the needed changes.
Step 9:   Retest and re-evaluate your hydrogen fuel cell design.
Step 10:   Share your results.

Terminology You Should Know

electrode: a conductor through which electricity enters or leaves an object

hydrogen: a highly flammable, colorless element; the lightest gas and most abundant element in the universe

potential energy: the stored energy an object has because of its position, rather than its motion

volt meter: an instrument for measuring electric potential in volts

voltage: the difference in electrical potential energy between two places in a circuit; measured in volts

Materials You May Need

- 12 inches platinum-coated nickel wire
- one 16-penny nail
- 9-volt battery with battery clip
- tape (transparent)
- 8 oz. glass of water
- volt meter
- popsicle stick

Task Requirements

1. <u>Research</u>: A one- to two-page paper summarizing your research on fuel cells and hydrogen fuel cells. Cite your sources. Your paper may include two pictures.
2. <u>Model</u>: A labeled drawing of your hydrogen fuel cell and explanation of your strategy.
3. <u>Results</u>: A record, analysis, and interpretation of test results.
4. <u>Conclusion</u>: A summary of the task and what actually happened. It should include the purpose, a brief description of the test procedure, and explanation of results.
5. <u>Reflection</u>: Think about your team's choices and your hydrogen fuel cell design. Then complete the "Reflection" handout.
6. <u>Evaluation</u>: Think about your behavior and performance as a team member. Then complete the "Self-Evaluation Rubric."

Calorimeter

Task: Design a simple calorimeter to measure how much energy is contained in various biomass food materials.

What You Should Know

Biomass is fuel developed from organic materials to create electricity or other forms of power. Biomass materials contain stored energy. The burning of these materials is a way of measuring their energy content. A calorimeter is an object used for measuring the heat of chemical reactions or physical changes as well as heat capacity.

Terminology You Should Know

calorie: the unit of thermal energy it takes to raise the temperature of one gram of water one degree Celsius

fossil fuel: the fuel formed from the remains of ancient plants and animals that can be burned to produce energy

heat: the transfer of thermal energy between substances that are at different temperatures

renewable energy: any energy source that is naturally replenished, such as solar, wind, geothermal, biomass, or hydroelectricity

Steps to Follow

Work with a team to complete the steps listed below. A team will have 3 or 4 members.

Step 1: Research biomass energy and calorimetry.
Step 2: Brainstorm ideas about how you might make a calorimeter.
Step 3: Draw a diagram of your calorimeter.
Step 4: Construct your calorimeter.
Step 5: Test your calorimeter.
Step 6: Evaluate the performance of your calorimeter.
Step 7: Identify how to improve the design of your calorimeter.
Step 8: Make the needed changes.
Step 9: Retest and re-evaluate your calorimeter design.
Step 10: Share your results.

Materials You Will Need

- biomass foods to test (peanuts, etc.)
- matches or lighter (use with adult supervision)
- empty soda can
- large coffee can (remove top and bottom)
- metal coat hanger
- graduated cylinder
- triple-beam balance
- Celsius thermometer
- paper clips
- cork

Task Requirements

1. <u>Research</u>: A one- to two-page paper summarizing your research on biomass energy and calorimetry. Cite your sources. Your paper may include two pictures.
2. <u>Model</u>: A labeled drawing of your calorimeter design and explanation of your strategy.
3. <u>Results</u>: A record, analysis, and interpretation of test results.
4. <u>Conclusions</u>: A summary of the task and what actually happened. It should include the purpose, a brief description of the test procedure, and explanation of results.
5. <u>Reflection</u>: Think about your team's choices and the design of your calorimeter. Then complete the "Reflection" handout.
6. <u>Evaluation</u>: Think about your behavior and performance as a team member. Then complete the "Self-Evaluation Rubric."

Recycling

Task: Design a system to separate and sort recyclable materials that might be sent to a recovery facility.

What You Should Know

In many neighborhoods, people place their recyclables at the curb. The collection trucks then haul the waste to a materials recovery facility (MRF) for processing. The materials are dumped on conveyor belts and multiple procedures (manual and mechanical) are used to separate the recyclable materials in the waste stream.

Materials You May Need

- assorted types and sizes of paper
- assorted plastic containers
- assorted cans (aluminum cans, aerosol, and other steel cans)
- paper clips
- bits of wire
- large magnet
- wide shallow pan
- water
- box fan

Terminology You Should Know

MRF (materials recovery facility): a facility for sorting, separating, and processing trash and recyclables

recycle: to reuse

Steps to Follow

Work with a team to complete the steps listed below. A team will have 3 or 4 members.

Step 1: Research recycling to discover the methods used to sort and separate recyclable materials.

Step 2: Test materials to determine which can be sorted by hand, flotation, magnetism, or blower method.

Step 3: Brainstorm ideas about how you might design a recovery system.

Step 4: Draw a diagram of your system by combining any of the procedures tested or procedures discovered in your research.

Step 5: Test, evaluate, and make the needed changes to your recovery system.

Step 6: Retest and re-evaluate your recovery system design.

Step 7: Share your results.

Task Requirements

1. Research: A one- to two-page paper summarizing your research on recycling and citing your sources. Your paper may include two pictures.
2. Model: A labeled drawing of your recyclable materials recovery system and explanation of your strategy.
3. Results: A record, analysis, and interpretation of test results.
4. Conclusion: A summary of the task and what actually happened. It should include the purpose, a brief description of the test procedure, and explanation of results.
5. Reflection: Think about your team's choice of recovery procedures and the order of the procedures in the system. Then complete the "Reflection" handout.
6. Evaluation: Think about your behavior and performance as a team member. Then complete the "Self-Evaluation Rubric."

Oil Spill Clean-Up

Task: Design a system to contain and clean up an oil spill in a body of water.

What You Should Know

A coastal area that is contaminated by an oil spill is never completely cleaned; the ecosystem takes several years to rehabilitate and may never return to its pre-spill state.

Steps to Follow

Work with a team to complete the steps listed below. A team will have 3 or 4 members.

Step 1:   Research oil spill prevention and methods used for cleaning up oil contamination.

Step 2:   Brainstorm ideas about methods that might work best for recovering the most oil from the water.

Step 3:   Draw a diagram of your oil recovery system.

Step 4:   Construct your system.

Step 5:   Test your system.

Step 6:   Evaluate your system.

Step 7:   Identify how to improve your system.

Step 8:   Make the needed changes.

Step 9:   Retest and re-evaluate your system.

Step 10: Share your results.

Terminology You Should Know

Archimedes' Principle: the law states that a body immersed in a fluid experiences a buoyant force equal to the weight of the fluid it displaces

buoyancy: the tendency of certain objects to float or rise in fluid

fluid: a substance, either liquid or gas, that can flow

sorbents: materials that are good at absorbing liquids

Materials You May Need

- newspaper
- plastic garbage bag
- graduated cylinders
- bowls or containers
- cotton balls
- measuring cup
- coffee filters
- paper towels
- water
- motor oil
- liquid soap
- straw or hay
- scissors

Task Requirements

1. <u>Research</u>: A one- to two-page paper summarizing your research on oil spill prevention and methods used for cleaning up oil contamination. Cite your sources. Your paper may include two pictures.

2. <u>Model</u>: A labeled drawing of your oil spill clean-up system and explanation of your strategy.

3. <u>Results</u>: A record, analysis, and interpretation of test results.

4. <u>Conclusion</u>: A summary of the task and what actually happened. It should include the purpose, a brief description of the test procedure, and explanation of results.

5. <u>Reflection</u>: Think about your team's choice of methods and about the design of your oil spill clean-up system. Then complete the "Reflection" handout.

6. <u>Evaluation</u>: Think about your behavior and performance as a team member. Then complete the "Self-Evaluation Rubric."

Vermicomposting System

Task: As a classroom, design a vermicomposting system for your school cafeteria. (Before getting started, contact your local health department concerning restrictions or guidelines for such a project.)

What You Should Know

Composting is good for the environment. Everyday leftover food from the school cafeteria is scraped into the garbage and transported to the local landfill. Composting helps minimize the pollution created by the trash in the landfill.

Terminology You Should Know

greenhouse gas: a gas that contributes to the greenhouse effect

vermicomposting: the practice of using worms to break down food scraps

worm: a creeping or burrowing invertebrate with long, slender, soft body and no limbs

Steps to Follow

Work with your classmates to complete the steps listed below.

Step 1: Research vermicomposting systems, worms and worm care, composting, and landfills.
Step 2: Brainstorm ideas about how you might design your system. Consider temperature, moisture, and ventilation for the worm bin.
Step 3: Draw a diagram of your system.
Step 4: Construct a model of your system.
Step 5: Test your system.
Step 6: Evaluate the performance of your vermicomposting system.
Step 7: Identify how to improve your design.
Step 8: Make the needed changes.
Step 9: Retest and re-evaluate your system.
Step 10: Share your results.

Materials You May Need

- supplies to build a wooden worm bin
- shredded paper (newsprint, paper bags, cardboard, or office paper—no glossy paper or magazines)
- composted animal manure (cow, horse, or rabbit)
- shredded, decaying leaves; peat moss
- food scraps (vegetables, fruits, eggshells, coffee grounds, paper coffee filters, and shredded garden waste)
- area on the school grounds to build a worm bin
- water
- red worms

Task Requirements

1. <u>Research</u>: A one- to two-page paper summarizing your research on vermicomposting systems, worms and worm care, composting, and landfills. Cite your sources. Your paper may include two pictures.
2. <u>Model</u>: A labeled drawing of your vermicomposting system and explanation of your strategy.
3. <u>Results</u>: A record, analysis, and interpretation of test results.
4. <u>Conclusions</u>: A summary of the task and what actually happened. It should include the purpose, a brief description of the test procedure, and explanation of results.
5. <u>Reflection</u>: Think about the design of your system. Then complete the "Reflection" handout.
6. <u>Evaluation</u>: Think about your behavior and performance as a team member. Then complete the "Self-Evaluation Rubric."

Water Purification System

Task: Design a water purification system that includes the first four steps typically used by water treatment plants: aeration, coagulation, sedimentation, and filtration. Note: Since your system will not include the last step, disinfection, your water will not be safe to drink.

What You Should Know

Surface water often contains impurities that make it look and smell bad. The water can also contain microorganisms that can cause sickness and disease.

Steps to Follow

Work with a team to complete the steps listed below. A team will have 3 or 4 members.

Step 1: Research water treatment processes, water filtration, and source water.

Step 2: Brainstorm ideas about how you might design a filtration system that will eliminate as much dirt as possible from a water sample you have been provided.

Step 3: Draw a diagram of your system.

Step 4: Construct a model of your system.

Step 5: Test your system.

Step 6: Evaluate the performance of your system.

Step 7: Identify how to improve your design and then make changes.

Step 8: Retest and re-evaluate your design.

Step 9: Share your results.

Terminology You Should Know

aeration: a process that adds air to water and allows gases trapped in the water to escape

coagulation: the process that allows dirt and other suspended particles to chemically stick together

filtration: the act of passing a gas or liquid through a porous material in order to separate the fluid from suspended particulate matter

sedimentation: the process of particles in the suspension settling out of the fluid

Materials You May Need

- water sample: two liters water with one cup soil added
- alum (add to aerated water to cause coagulation)
- four two-liter plastic bottles with caps
- rubber bands
- tablespoon and stirring spoon
- large beaker
- filter material (choose four): cotton balls, cheesecloth, coffee filter, fine sand, coarse sand, wire screen, aquarium gravel, rocks, paper

Task Requirements

1. Research: A one- to two-page paper summarizing your research of water treatment processes, water filtration, and source water. Cite your sources. Your paper may include two pictures.
2. Model: A labeled drawing of your design and explanation of your strategy.
3. Results: A record, analysis, and interpretation of test results.
4. Conclusions: A summary of the task and what actually happened. It should include the purpose, a brief description of the test procedure, and explanation of results.
5. Reflection: Think about your team's choice of methods and about your water purification system design. Then complete the "Reflection" handout.
6. Evaluation: Think about your behavior and performance as a team member. Then complete the "Self-Evaluation Rubric."

Tornado-Proof Housing

Task: Design a shelter that can withstand high winds and protect people from the forces of a tornado.

What You Should Know

Each year tornadoes in Tornado Alley cause thousands of dollars of damage. Ninety percent of these are EF3 or less in intensity. New innovations in home and building design are being tested to withstand 165 mph winds from a tornado.

Terminology You Should Know

air pressure: the weight of air

anemometer: an instrument used to measure the wind speed in miles per hour

barometer: an instrument used to measure changes in air pressure

tornado: a violent, whirling wind that moves across the ground in a narrow path

Materials You May Need

- large fan with three settings
- design materials: to be determined by students through their research

Steps to Follow

Work with a team to complete the steps listed below. A team will have 3 or 4 members.

Step 1: Research an area where tornadoes have a disastrous impact on housing. Identify local building materials, traditional housing design, and possible storm intensity.

Step 2: Brainstorm ideas about how you might design a sturdy shelter.

Step 3: Draw a diagram of your shelter.

Step 4: Construct a model of your shelter.

Step 5: Test your shelter model.

Step 6: Evaluate your shelter model.

Step 7: Identify how to improve your shelter design.

Step 8: Make the needed changes.

Step 9: Retest and re-evaluate your design.

Step 10: Share your results.

Task Requirements

1. <u>Research</u>: A one- to two-page paper summarizing your research on tornadoes and housing design. Cite your sources. Your paper may include two pictures.
2. <u>Model</u>: A labeled drawing of your shelter design and explanation of your strategy.
3. <u>Results</u>: A record, analysis, and interpretation of test results.
4. <u>Conclusion</u>: A summary of the task and what actually happened. It should include the purpose, a brief description of the test procedure, and explanation of results.
5. <u>Reflection</u>: Think about your team's choices and your shelter design. Then complete the "Reflection" handout.
6. <u>Evaluation</u>: Think about your behavior and performance as a team member. Then complete the "Self-Evaluation Rubric."

Beach Erosion

Task: Design a model that would reduce beachfront erosion.

What You Should Know

Beaches are slowly disappearing due to coastal erosion. There are many factors that influence erosion, including severe storms. Shoreline structures are built to alter the effects of ocean waves, currents, and sand movement, thus reducing the loss of beachfront sand. Some of these structures actually do more harm than good, however.

Steps to Follow

Work with a team to complete the steps listed below. A team will have 3 or 4 members.

Step 1: Research coastline erosion and solutions.
Step 2: Brainstorm ideas about how you might solve the problem.
Step 3: Draw a diagram of your model.
Step 4: Construct your beach erosion model.
Step 5: Test your model.
Step 6: Evaluate your model.
Step 7: Identify how to improve your beach erosion model.
Step 8: Make the needed changes.
Step 9: Retest and re-evaluate your erosion reduction model.
Step 10: Share your results.

Terminology You Should Know

coastal erosion: a natural process that removes sediment from shorelines

ocean waves: an area of moving water that is raised above the main surface of an ocean, usually generated by wind on the ocean's surface

prevailing currents: the ocean currents most frequently observed during a given period, such as a month, a season, or a year

sea level: the level of the ocean's surface

tides: the rising and falling of the surface of the ocean caused twice daily by the attraction of the sun and the moon

Materials You May Need

- Materials to be determined by students through their research

Task Requirements

1. <u>Research</u>: A one- to two-page paper summarizing your research on coastal erosion and solutions. Cite your sources. Your paper may include two pictures.
2. <u>Model</u>: A labeled drawing of your model and explanation of your strategy.
3. <u>Results</u>: A record, analysis, and interpretation of test results.
4. <u>Conclusion</u>: A summary of the task and what actually happened. It should include the purpose, a brief description of the test procedure, and explanation of results.
5. <u>Reflection</u>: Think about your team's choices and your beach erosion model. Then complete the "Reflection" handout.
6. <u>Evaluation</u>: Think about your behavior and performance as a team member. Then complete the "Self-Evaluation Rubric."

Greenhouse Effect

Task: Design a model that will demonstrate the effect of greenhouse gases on Earth's atmosphere.

What You Should Know

For the last century, the main source of energy has been fossil fuels. The gases formed by the burning of these fuels are building up in the atmosphere. They act like greenhouse glass. The result, experts believe, is Earth heating up and undergoing global warming.

Steps to Follow

Work with a team to complete the steps listed below. A team will have 3 or 4 members.

Step 1:   Research the greenhouse effect and global warming.

Step 2:   Brainstorm ideas about how you might design your model to show the effects of greenhouse gases.

Step 3:   Draw a diagram of your model.

Step 4:   Construct your model.

Step 5:   Test your model.

Step 6:   Evaluate the performance of your model.

Step 7:   Identify how to improve the design of your model.

Step 8:   Make the needed changes to your model.

Step 9:   Retest and re-evaluate your model.

Step 10: Share your results.

Terminology You Should Know

atmosphere: the layer of gases surrounding the earth

climate: the average weather pattern of a region

global warming: the rise in the earth's temperature due to an increased greenhouse effect

greenhouse effect: the heating caused by atmospheric gases trapping heat at the earth's surface

Materials You May Need

- flexible straws
- tape
- thermometers
- ice cubes
- plastic wrap
- scissors
- clock
- sunny day

Task Requirements

1. <u>Research</u>: A one- to two-page paper summarizing your research on the greenhouse effect and global warming. Cite your sources. Your paper may include two pictures.
2. <u>Model</u>: A labeled drawing of your model design and explanation of your strategy.
3. <u>Results</u>: A record, analysis, and interpretation of test results.
4. <u>Conclusion</u>: A summary of the task and what actually happened. It should include the purpose, a brief description of the test procedure, and explanation of results.
5. <u>Reflection</u>: Think about your team's choices and the design of your greenhouse effect model. Then complete the "Reflection" handout.
6. <u>Evaluation</u>: Think about your behavior and performance as a team member. Then complete the "Self-Evaluation Rubric."

Green Roof

Task: Design a "green roof" for an urban building that will slow runoff, ease the urban heat island effect, and increase building insulation.

What You Should Know

Many urban buildings have rooftop gardens or "green roofs." Green roof systems provide many benefits, including the reduction of energy costs.

Steps to Follow

Work with a team to complete the steps listed below. A team will have 3 or 4 members.

Step 1: Research green roof technology and urban heat islands.

Step 2: Brainstorm ideas about how you might design a green roof. Consider the three layers of a green roof: a vapor barrier; soil/gravel/growing medium; and plants.

Step 3: Draw a diagram of your roof design.

Step 4: Construct your roof design.

Step 5: Test your roof design.

Step 6: Evaluate the performance of your roof design.

Step 7: Identify how to improve the design of your roof.

Step 8: Make the needed changes.

Step 9: Retest and re-evaluate your roof design.

Terminology You Should Know

heat: the transfer of thermal energy between substances that are at different temperatures

photosynthesis: the food-making process in green plants that uses sunlight

stormwater runoff: the water that flows over the ground surface into the sewer system

urban heat islands: the temperature discrepancy between cities and surrounding rural areas due to human activities

Materials You May Need

- shoe boxes with lids
- soil/gravel/growing medium
- tar paper
- strong, double-sided tape
- sod/plants
- scissors
- thermometer
- heat lamp
- timer

Task Requirements

1. Research: A one- to two-page paper summarizing your research on green roof technology and urban heat islands. Cite your sources. Your paper may include two pictures.

2. Model: A labeled drawing of your green roof design and explanation of your strategy.

3. Results: A record, analysis, and interpretation of test results.

4. Conclusion: A summary of the task and what actually happened. It should include the purpose, a brief description of the test procedure, and explanation of results.

5. Reflection: Think about your team's choices and your green roof design. Then complete the "Reflection" handout.

6. Evaluation: Think about your behavior and performance as a team member. Then complete the "Self-Evaluation Rubric."

Hydroponics: Grow Green

Task: Design a hydroponics system that will grow lettuce seed.

What You Should Know

Hydroponics is a method of growing plants using mineral nutrient solutions in water without soil. Hydroponics is especially beneficial to people who have poor soil or no soil at all. Hydroponic farming gives the grower the ability to grow higher-yielding crops without using large amounts of pesticides.

Steps to Follow

Work with a team to complete the steps listed below. A team will have 3 or 4 members.

Step 1:   Research plants, hydroponics, and hydroponic systems.
Step 2:   Brainstorm ideas about how you might design a hydroponic system.
Step 3:   Draw a diagram of your system.
Step 4:   Construct your system.
Step 5:   Test your system.
Step 6:   Evaluate the performance of your system.
Step 7:   Identify how to improve the design of your system.
Step 8:   Make the needed changes.
Step 9:   Retest and re-evaluate your system design.
Step 10: Share your results.

Terminology You Should Know

aggregate: an inert substance such as sand, gravel, small stones, vermiculite, or perlite

capillary action: the process that plants use to pull water up from the ground

hydroponics: the growing of plants without soil

nutrient: a substance that an organism needs in order to survive and grow

photosynthesis: the food-making process in green plants that uses sunlight

Materials You May Need

- Materials to be determined by students through their research

Task Requirements

1. Research: A one- to two-page paper summarizing your research on plants, hydroponics, and hydroponics systems. Cite your sources. Your paper may include two pictures.
2. Model: A labeled drawing of your hydroponic system design and explanation of your strategy.
3. Results: A record, analysis, and interpretation of test results.
4. Conclusion: A summary of the task and what actually happened. It should include the purpose, a brief description of the test procedure, and explanation of results.
5. Reflection: Think about your team's choices and your hydroponic system design. Then complete the "Reflection" handout.
6. Evaluation: Think about your behavior and performance as a team member. Then complete the "Self-Evaluation Rubric."